1 MONTH OF
FREE
READING

at

www.ForgottenBooks.com

By purchasing this book you are eligible for one month membership to ForgottenBooks.com, giving you unlimited access to our entire collection of over 1,000,000 titles via our web site and mobile apps.

To claim your free month visit:
www.forgottenbooks.com/free918998

ISBN 978-0-266-98299-9
PIBN 10918998

For support please visit www.forgottenbooks.com

NORMAL SCHOOL BULLETIN

PUBLISHED BY THE EASTERN ILLINOIS STATE NORMAL SCHOOL

Entered March 5, as second-class matter at the postoffice at Charleston, Illinois, Act of Congress, July 16, 1894.

CHARLESTON, ILLINOIS, October 1, 1908.   No. 23

SOME PROBLEMS IN EDUCATION. *

By JOHN M. COULTER, PH. D.

Professor and Head of the Department of Botany, The University of Chicago.

Never in the history of education in America has there been such a universal movement towards change as now. Conscious that existing plans must be modified, all who are interested in education have a feeling of great unrest, and this feeling expresses itself at every educational conference. Discussions are endless, and often apparently fruitless, for opinions are as numerous as are the factors of the problem, and the mighty power of what *has been* over the frail form of what *might be* holds us with a death-like grip.

It is not probable that some great educational reformer will arise and lead us directly to the truth. In these days we are all searching for the truth so eagerly that it is not likely to come as a sudden revelation. It will probably come by a series of approximations, and it will not be recognized until it has been thoroughly tested; and when it is known and acknowledged, no one can tell who has been responsible for it, for it will have been evolved gradually from all our former

*An address delivered before the Eastern Illinois Teachers' Association, Oct. 16, 1908.

experience. There is no problem concerning which w
so ill afford to be dogmatic; and no one concerning whic
are so dogmatically inclined. There is no question con
ing which past experience may be so unsafe a guide,
what we have attained cannot be compared with what we
for and have a right to expect. There is no problem in v
theorizing may lead so far astray, and no problem whic
been so covered up with crude theorizing.

We do not understand the structure we are seeki
develop; we do not know what we want to do for it whe
shall understand it; and we do not know how to accom
when we shall know what we want. Out of this mass o
gations we are constructing our hypotheses, and even
ture to hope that they may stand. That student of educ
has not advanced very far into his subject who has any
measure of confidence in his own opinions, or in those o
one else. The effect of all this should be, not a discour
but a receptive mind; not dogmatism, but liberality.

There need be no expectation that the true educat
just at hand, and those impatient souls who cannot res
tent until everything is settled, must cultivate the scie
spirit, which has learned to labor and to wait. It is n'
a fact, however, that the true education is approaching
that its coming will be hastened in proportion to our c
isfaction with the existing order of things, and our rej
of that mind-benumbing dogma that the past contains a
is best in education. Our educational growth should l
that of a vigorous tree, rooted and grounded in all the
that the past has revealed, but stretching out its br:
and ever-renewed foliage to the air and the sunshin
taking into its life the forces of to-day.

The test of teaching is the *result*. As one exami
product of the schools today, has he a right to feel sa
The essential feature of the test is not to be obtaine
school records, but from our social order. Are we co
ing to society men and women who will improve it
and women who are not only sound morally, but wl

wide interests and are sane? Have we made them incapable of becoming victims of demagoguery, of superstition, of hallucinations of any kind? It has seemed to me that our educational schemes lack efficiency in just this direction; and that, judged by the results, we have not hit upon just the form of training that results in sanity among the greatest number of adults.

It may be that my experience in a great center of cosmopolitan population has exaggerated the situation in my own mind; but that such centers will become larger, more numerous, and more commanding seems certain. One of our fundamental problems, therefore, is to develop an attitude of mind that demands truth before action, that knows how to uncover truth and to recognize it, and that maintains the judicial equipoise until the facts are in.

I cannot presume to claim a solution to this problem, and I believe that no one can; for such problems are only recognized as solved when the results appear. And yet, with such a definite purpose in view, all suggestions that can be made to appear reasonable are worth consideration. In my judgment a larger development of the scientific spirit should have a strong tendency toward solving this problem. The scientific spirit is a certain attitude of mind, some of whose characteristics are as follows:

(1) *It is a spirit of inquiry.* In our experience we encounter a vast body of beliefs of all kinds, from trivial to important. We can recognize that this is composed of two elements: (1) the priceless results of generations of experience and (2) heirloom rubbish. The scientific spirit seeks to investigate these beliefs and to discover the truth that is mixed with the rubbish. The world needs a going over of its stock in trade now and then; not all at once, or once for all, but gradually as knowledge becomes more generally diffused. The scientific spirit certainly has nothing in common with dogmatism, but implies an open mind, a teachable disposition, and a responsive will.

(2) *It demands an evident connection between an effect and*

its claimed cause. It is really in the laboratory tha⸱
to appreciate what constitutes proof. Most pec
have the idea that every effect may be explained
factor operating as a cause; when the few simpl⸱
have been analysed show numerous factors inte
way so complicated as to be bewildering. In wh⸱
must we be in such enormously complex subjects ε
order, politics, education, and religion? I presu
are as yet playing with the fringes of these gre
and that all our conclusions are largely empirical
tain that here demagoguery gets in its siniste
leads the unwary millions astray.

(3) *It keeps close to the facts.* One of my n
problems as a teacher is to check students who a
fact and then disappear in a flight of fancy thε
prodigious. Of course additional facts check this
for flight in one direction is checked by a pull in
direction. Most people, however, are so unhampe
that flight is free. It seems to be a general imp⸱
one may start with a single fact, and by some logⁱ
ery construct an elaborate system of belief and |
authentic conclusion; much as it was once in
Cuvier could reconstruct an animal were a sing
sented to him. A fact is without influence exce⸱
immediate vicinity. Facts are like stepping sto
has a reasonably close series of them, he may mε
in a given direction; but if he steps beyond them l
The influence of a fact diminishes as the distan
like the rays of light from a candle, until the var
is reached; but the whole structure of many ε
beyond the vanishing point. Such vain imagi
seductive charm for many people, whose life anc
even shaped by them. This emotional insanity of
ades under the name of "subtle thinking;" not
if it means thinking without any material for t
active mind turned in upon itself, without any vε
tive material, is apt to result in mental chaos.

There must be a saner product from our educational system; minds with such poise that they do not lose their balance; with such training that no mirage can be mistaken for a reality. To me this seems to be the greatest of all our problems; how to produce rational, sane citizens in such numbers that they will dominate.

From among other problems I wish to select certain ones that have thrust themselves recently upon my attention. Naturally, my experience and yours may not have been the same in reference to these matters; but if they do not happen to be pertinent to your experience they will serve to illus-trate conditions elsewhere.

Since leaving a state institution, I have had little occa-sion to visit high schools; but in the last few months I have had opportunity to renew my first-hand acquaintance with some of them. I recognized that during the last sixteen years we have been making tremendous progress in educa-tional ideals and technique, and that in this general progress the high schools must have shared. I was not disappointed in this belief, for I discovered that in material equipment, in greater freedom and variety of work, in the closer articu-lation of work to the necessities and obligations of life, there has been very great progress. No student of education can fail to see in all this a genuine and most gratifying progress; and yet there are certain things that seem to me worthy of consideration, in fact quite fundamental.

I. The Act of Teaching.

There seems to be still a great deal of ineffective teach-ing. That there may be no misunderstanding, I hasten to say that there is more poor teaching in universities than in high schools, and the larger the university, the larger does the percentage of poor teaching become. This would be disastrous in higher education, were it not compensated for by the high schools, which turn over to the universities ma-terial that can stand the shock of a certain amount of poor teaching. There is an excuse for this in the universities

which does not obtain in the high schools, and it is so ev
dent that I do not need to specify it. There is all the mor
reason, therefore, that the high schools should bring th
technique of teaching to its greatest efficiency.

I do not refer to the subject-matter or to the equipmer
of the school in material things, but simply to the contact c
teacher and pupil in the act of teaching. We construct
well-ordered machine that runs smoothly, and then at th
point of application often get no power, and the trouble
so subtle that correction seems almost impossible. To catc
by observation the qualities of an effective teacher is lik
trying to catch a personality. For such a one no rules ca
be formulated. He is like the real artist, born with a feelin
for his work. And yet there are certain obvious things tha
can be observed, and these ought to be helpful.

Perhaps the most difficult work of the teacher is to aj
preciate the exact mental condition of the pupil in referenc
to any subject. Unless there is complete adaptation in th
regard, the contact is a failure, leading to mutual disgu;
and distrust.

In much of the teaching I have observed in the school
the impression left upon me has been one of astonishin
lack of simplicity and directness in the presentation of su
jects, resulting in utter confusion. My own conclusion h;
been that this indicates either ignorance of the subject, (
lack of teaching ability, or a wooden application of son
pedagogical refinement which has been learned somewher
and which is either not worth applying in any case, or
wofully misplaced. Hardly can there be imagined a wor
combination than wooden teaching by one ignorant of t
subject. In a great mass of teaching, instead of using cle
expression and direct presentation, the effort seems to be
use most unusual phrases, as far from an ordinary vocab
lary as possible, and to approach the subject in such a d
vious way that its significance is in danger of being misse
The philosophy of teaching is well enough as a backgroun
but philosophical teaching is usually out of place. To inje

the abstractions and phrase-making of normal training into the school room is to dismiss clearness and all intellectual contact with pupils. This is no criticism of pedagogial training, for I would be the last to suggest that any profession should be attempted without professional training; but it is a criticism of those teachers who do not known how to apply their training, and follow what they regard to be rules, rather than principles.

Probably the greatest factor in this result is the fact that far too many teachers have learned more of the form of teaching than of the subject matter to be taught. There is no flexibility, no power of adaptation, no ability to depart from a fixed routine, and hence no adjustment to the very diverse mental conditions they must meet and are expected to stimulate. Necessary flexibility in method is impossible without a broad grasp of the subject to be presented. The amount of meaningless drudgery that this senseless formalism has forced upon pupils has long been recognized by parents, whose indignation occasionally breaks out in condemnation of the schools as places where method has run to seed.

It is very fortunate that the human mind is so tough a structure that it will develop in spite of teachers, and all of our educational experiments have not succeeeed in sensibly stunting it. I have about concluded that the great problem in the act of teaching is not how to impart instruction, but how to oppose the fewest obstacles to mental development. The human mind has a mighty way of overcoming obstacles, but, as teachers, we have no right to attempt to make them insurmountable. I have almost cried out in indignation when witnessing some pupil whose quick mind has discovered short cuts to results, ruthlessly forced upon the procrustean bed of method by some teacher who knows only one way. It is such things that bring the profession into deserved contempt, as one that has not yet emerged from blind empiricism.

I know that this is imposing a tremendous burden of preparation upon teachers, but how is it to be avoided? In no part of educational work is flexibility in presentation and in material so necessary as at its beginning. Truth is many-sided, and it is always a question as to which side shall be presented. The teacher who knows only one side is hopeless.

The whole situation results in a kind of paradox. If teachers develop such a grasp of the subject as to handle it with the greatest flexibility, will ordinary school positions content them? The question can be answered in only one way, and therefore we must come to this way sooner or later. The schools must be recognized as the greatest opportunity for *teaching*, as the universities are recognized as the greatest opportunity for *research*; and positions in the two must become equal in public esteem, in scholarly esteem, and in income.

II. THE RELATION OF UNIVERSITY TRAINING TO HIGH SCHOOL INSTRUCTION.

This topic grows out of the last one, and in fact is a part of it, but it seems to need special mention. The high schools have developed to the point where not only university training but often graduate training is demanded of the teachers. This is inevitable and desirable, for it will secure that grasp of the subject and facility in using it that were spoken of under the previous topic. It is to become increasingly true that the great field of our university masters and doctors is the high school; for they are becoming too numerous to provide for in any other way. Comparatively few of them can find places in universities and colleges; and most of those who do would be better off in good high schools. The lot of an assistant in a university or even a professor in a small college is not so happy as it may look from the outside. In the former position, promotion is apt to be exasperatingly slow; while in the latter position it is impossible.

All this means that there is to be an increasingly large injection of university trained men and women into the high schools, and on account of this we are confronted by a distinct educational danger. I have noticed a distinct tendency on the part of teachers so trained to transfer the methods of the university into the high schools, which goes so far, in some cases, as to duplicate the elementary courses of universities. In my judgment nothing could be more out of place in a high school, where the university atmosphere is a distinct disadvantage. There must be developed a clear understanding that the university training is to give to the high school teacher a grasp of the subject, but not at all a method of presentation. Such factors as the maturity of the pupil, the time at command, the size of classes, the purpose, all differ in the two cases, and presentation becomes a totally different problem.

I grant it is easier to *repeat* a course than to *construct* one; but the teacher's problem is a constructive one, for it involves the power to *initiate* rather than the ability to *imitate*. It seems to be a hard lesson for university graduates to learn, that a high school is not a college, and that it demands its own peculiar kind of teaching.

Naturally my attention has been directed especially to the instruction in science, and I have been amazed to see the large number of miniature college laboratories organized in high schools. The laboratories are well enough, but the courses given in them are college courses.

I recognize that probably no subject has been more discussed than science in secondary schools. School teachers and university teachers, in committees and conventions and addresses and periodicals have wrestled with this problem. The school teachers knew their pupils and their facilities, but not too much about the subjects. The university teachers knew the subjects, but very little about the pupils, and still less about the facilities. It was hard for both to occupy the same standpoint, and both were inclined to be somewhat dogmatic, the university teacher perhaps a little the more so. School patrons, with their demands, have been a factor also.

The sciences are all in a state of extremely rapid evolution, and the schools are often finding themselves strangely at variance with the universities, and are plainly and repeatedly told that their science is an absurdity. These unpleasant statements are usually received with becoming meekness, as coming from those who are supposed to know, but they have led to nothing or to chaos.

This situation has been intensified by the numerous textbooks and laboratory guides, bearing the favorite legend, "for high schools and colleges," and written by college men, from the college standpoint, which calculates upon time and equipment and a reasonable amount of intellectual maturity. I must not be misunderstood, for I believe that these books are immensely useful, as keeping current the material and the point of view. My criticism is directed against the too slavish use of them. They are designed, or they ought to be designed, to simplify the problem of material for the teacher, but beyond that lies the teacher's own problem of presentation, which no one else can assume to solve.

In my judgment, therefore, there should be included in the preparation of the university graduate, who proposes to teach in the high schools, a study of the conditions and purposes of these schools, especially with reference to the differences in the factors entering into the educational ideals of high schools and of universities. Unless this is done, the the majority of university graduates will attempt to repeat their university courses in the high schools. The minority are the born teachers, who adapt instruction to pupil and material instinctively; but they will always be in the minority.

The problem is in the hands of the high school teachers, for it cannot be solved by any schemes imposed upon them from the outside. They may look elsewhere for material and for suggestions; but the important features of the problem do not enter into the experience of the university instructor.

III. The Schools and the Universities.

This problem, so far from being solved, is getting into a condition so involved that its future status is very uncertain. Questions of entrance requirements, of examination or certificate, represent the border line problems that interest high schools and universities alike. As a rule, so far as the high schools are concerned, the state universities have determined these standards; and as a rule the other universities, in self defence, have followed them. From the standpoint of the university, the high school exists to prepare the university students. From the standpoint of the high school, its primary function may be somewhat different. The university, and especially the state university, cannot afford to disarticulate itself from the rest of the school system; on the other hand the high school cannot afford to lose the uplift of the university.

Universities, as a rule, are great storehouses of educational precedents, which have descended from mediaeval times, when there were very few subjects organized for study, and these few held little or no relation to the problems of intelligent living. They were the possession and pastime of a favored few. Heredity has filled the blood of most universities with this so-called scholastic spirit, so that they find it hard to adapt themselves to the new conditions. It should be remembered that the old selection of subjects was a matter of necessity rather than of choice; but since the opportunity for ample choice has come, the old necessity no longer exists, although it is the tendency of most universities to regard the older subjects and the older methods as possessing a peculiar relation to education.

On the other hand, the American school system is peculiarly a modern institution, developed out of the necessities of our own civilization, and seeking to meet the demands of the time. The schools are handicapped by no precedents, and have no heirloom rubbish to intercalate among their modern furniture. To the thoughtful student of education it is intensely interesting to watch the progress of the effort to articulate the very old, as represented by the universities, with the very new, as represented by the schools. It was necessary that it should lead to clashing opinions, and that the old and the new should scoff at one another.

The old had the advantage of that dignity and influence which belong to years and an honorable history; the new had the advantage of numbers and of public opinion. Neither could dictate to the other, although both wanted to. It is really quite remarkable that the two have gotten along so well together, and this argues well for the deep-rooted belief of each that it must have the other. In the main, however, the universities have imposed more upon the schools than they have conceded; as is very apt to be the case when the weight of educational authority is largely upon one side.

It is hard for the universities to lay aside the thought that the high schools are primarily preparatory schools. If this be conceded, then the universities must be permitted to dictate the courses of study. But it is not conceded, and still the universities have in effect dictated the courses. They have done it by making the entrance requirements so specific and so numerous that the four years of high school are absolutely filled with them. If there is anything for a high school to do besides preparing students for college, it either has no time for it or it is compelled to organize a separate and independent curriculum which does not lead to college. Most schools are so situated that they cannot do both. The colleges are honest in their opinion that their entrance requirements represent the very best education for a student of that grade, whether he is to enter college or not. I have helped express and enforce this opinion, and so cannot be accused of any prejudice if I now venture to dissent from it. I still think that a larger part of the university entrance requirement represents the very wisest subjects that can enter into the curriculum of the high school; but when these requirements become so large and so specific that they destroy the educational autonomy of the high school, and convert it into a university appendage, then I am constrained to dissent.

The increasing standards are to permit more advanced work in the university, and this is a magnificent purpose, to be encouraged by every true lover of education; but it must not be done at the expense of the schools, the great mass of whose students never enter the university. It is wise to introduce into the high school studies which may be of no special benefit to the pupil preparing for college, for·they are of great benefit to the lives of those whose educational career must end with the high school. As I understand it, the high school is intended to train for better citizenship, to enlarge the opportunity for obtaining a better livelihood, to open broader views of life and its duties. In order to be of the greatest benefit to the greatest number, its course of study must be constructed as though there were to be no further formal education for the pupil. Subjects must be related to the needs of life and society, but this need not and should not exclude those subjects or those methods which prepare and stimulate for further study; for there should be constant recognition of the fact that the secondary school is but an intermediate stage·in educational progress.

I regard the recent tendency of universities to increase their demands upon the schools as unwise, and as fraught with danger. It has long been my theory that the specific demands may be very few, and these so self-evident that a school would not be likely to omit them. What the universities need is not a specific kind of preparation, but a certain degree of intellectual development, a development which is usually much broader than that obtained from the average college preparation. I may be allowed to say, as the result of many years of experience, that this average college preparation presents to the universities the most narrow and unevenly trained material that can be imagined. Nowhere are the evils of specialization so apparent as in the entrance preparation demanded by many colleges. If this specialization results in comparatively poor college material, its results may be regarded as simply disastrous to the high school in its primary purpose. This is not a plea for a multiplication of studies in the high schools, for one of their great weaknesses today is their tremendously congested condition. It is a plea for the relief of this congestion by reducing the university demands, not in quantity, but in specific assignment, leaving the schools freer to exercise their own judgment in the selection of special subjects.

The time has long passed when any aristocracy of subjects has any right to claim the privilege of standing guard over every avenue leading to a higher education.   Any student who has successfully pursued a well-organized and coherent course for four years in a high school should be able to continue his work in the universities.   There are differences of opinion as to what constitutes a well-organized and coherent course, but it could be outlined by principles rather than in detail, and the schools themselves should be responsible for its construction.   A minimum of subjects and a maximum of time, continuous rather than scattered work, a range broad enough to touch upon all of the fundamental regions of work, methods that will secure precision in thought and expression, contact with the life and work of the times in which we are destined to live, are certainly principles that are sufficient, but concerning whose details none should dogmatize, for they may well vary with the teachers and with the local conditions.

The university should always be called upon for advice as to courses and methods, but it should be from the standpoint of the schools, a standpoint best determined by the schools themselves.   For instance, I would not presume to dictate to any school the way in which botany must be taught; but I would count it a privilege, upon being made acquainted with the preparation of the teacher, and the facilities at command, to suggest certain lines of work, from which, as a rational being, knowing the conditions better than any one else, he could make his choice.   I would regard it as my chief function to guard inexperience against waste of time and energy, rather than to direct specifically.   If the teacher does not know enough to make a choice in such matters, I would advise the selection of some other means of making a living.   I must confess to being a great stickler for individual independence and responsibility, and that school or that teacher which is held in the dictatorial grasp of some higher authority that permits no expression of individualism in methods, which sternly represses all spontaneity and originality, which demands an automaton-like service, is pedagogically blighted. The vast machinery of the schools which enters into every petty detail, rides them like an old man of the sea, and is converting schools into factories, and teachers into drudges.

And how shall well-prepared material be recognized at the university? Lately the entrance examination system has thrust itself upon my attention afresh. I do not know whether this ghost of a dead past stalks into your educational banquets or not, but it is rampant in certain universities that rather pride themselves upon being haunted. A better scheme to show how not to do it was never devised. At the present day it is pecular to the Chinese theory of education, and that nation should be allowed its exclusive use. It is both barbarous and unscientific. I would make no serious objection to its barbarity, if it were scientific; that is, if it obtained the information it seeks. What teacher does not recognize that the estimate of the ordinary examination must be tempered by knowledge of the daily work, or grave injustice may be done? How much greater the need of this tempering in the extraordinary entrance examination! If the tempering is necessary to obtain the facts, why not substitute the tempering entirely for the examination? Which means, of course, the substitution of the daily knowledge of the teacher for the ignorance of the university examiner. I wish no better evidence concerning the intellectual equipment of a candidate for entrance into a university than the judgment of the teachers with whom he has worked, for I can get no better, nor any other half so good.

It is strange that universities are more concerned about their raw material than about their finished product. If they would be a little less sensitive concerning entrance require ments, and a little more particular concerning graduation requirements it might be a better expenditure of energy. It has always seemed to me that the fine meshed seive is set at the wrong end of the university.

In conclusion, it must be repeated that no complete change in these matters which I have presented, and in others of equal importance, can come suddenly. We can be dissatisfied with the results, and can point out defects here and there which in our judgment are responsible for them, but certainly no single opinion should be followed. The subject is too vast in its importance and in its ramifications to be grasped by any one man. Its many sides confound our best judgment. It is always easy to rail at the existing order of things in a pessimistic way, and such railing is only productive of evil, but criticism, born of the intense love of the cause of education, and longing for its best development, is always helpful. Such thoughts are at work like leaven, and when they shall have permeated sufficiently, movements will begin, quietly and moderately it is to be hoped, but persistently, and out of the movements there will slowly arise new methods, which upon trial have met with general consent. No student of our educational institutions can fail to observe that the general progress toward better things recently has been very rapid, probably as rapid as is safe for wise organization. We can afford to be optimistic at the outlook, and need only concern ourselves with recognizing and attacking the points of weakness; some of which will always exist to give us occupation. There is within our educational system, not perfection, unless it be in its ultimate purpose, but a wonderful power of endless development. We are to establish an American system of education, not copied from ancient times nor from other countries, but drawing from them all that is appropriate; and, adding our own ideals, we are to meet conditions for which we find no precedent. To such great service are you called, and it will demand not only your enthusiastic and unselfish devotion to the cause of education, but your best thought and calmest judgment as educators, and your most competent work as teachers.

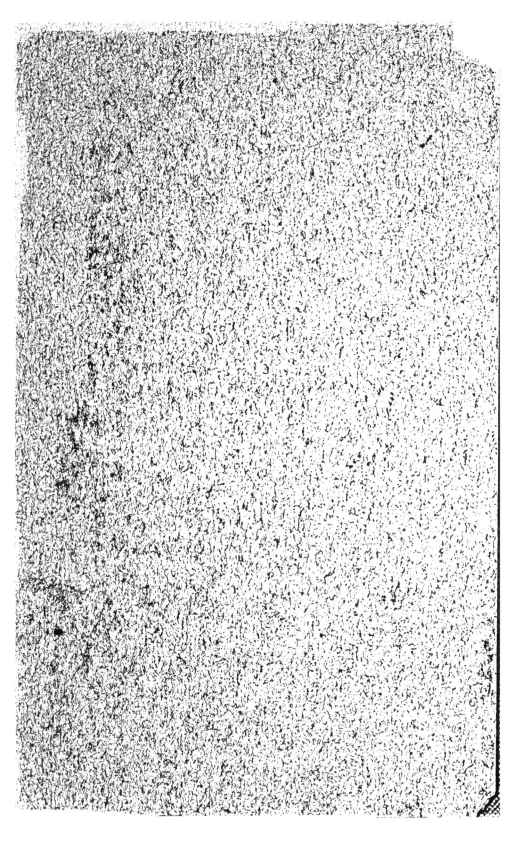

THE NORMAL

SCHOOL BULLETIN

UNIVERSITY OF ILLINOIS

PRESIDENT'S OFFICE

OCTOBER 1, 1909

EDUCATION AND UTILITY

BY

W. C. BAGLEY

JNIVERSITY OF ILLINOIS

PRESIDENT'S OFFICE

NORMAL SCHOOL BULLETIN

PUBLISHED BY THE EASTERN ILLINOIS STATE NORMAL SCHOOL

Entered March 5, as second-class matter at the postoffice at Charleston, Illinois, Act of Congress, July 16, 1894.

CHARLESTON, ILLINOIS, October 1, 1909.　　　　　　No. 26

*EDUCATION AND UTILITY**

By W. C. Bagley, Ph. D.

Director of the School of Education

University of Illinois

I wish to discuss with you this morning some phases of the problem that is perhaps foremost in the minds of the teaching public today: the problem, namely, of making education bear more directly and more effectively upon the work of practical, every-day life. I have no doubt that some of you feel, when this problem is suggested, very much as I felt when I first suggested to myself the possibility of discussing it with you. You may doubtless have heard some phases of this problem discussed at every meeting of this association for the past ten years—if you have been a member so long as that. Certain it is that we all grow weary of the reiteration of even the best of truths, but certain it is also that some problems are always before us, and until they are solved satisfactorily they will always stimulate men to devise means for their solution.

*Paper read before the Eastern Illinois Teachers Association, October 15, 1909.

I should say at the outset, however, that I shall not ; tempt to justify to this audience the introduction of vocatioɪ subjects into the elementary and secondary curriculum. shall take it for granted that you have already made up yc minds upon this matter. I shall not take your time an attempt to persuade you that agriculture ought to taught in the rural schools, or manual training and domes science in all schools. I am personally convinced of t value of such work and I shall take it for granted that y are likewise convinced.

My task today, then, is of another type. I wish to d cuss with you some of the implications of this matter of util in respect to the work that every elementary school is doi and always must do, no matter how much hand-work or ᴠ cational material it may introduce. My problem in otɪ words, concerns the ordinary subject-matter of the curriɛ lum,--reading and writing and arithmetic; geography, a grammar, and history,—those things which, like the poor, ɛ always with us, but which we seem a little ashamed to tɛ about in public. Truly, from reading the educational journ: and hearing educational discussion today, the layman miɡ well infer that what we term the "useful" education and t education that is now offered by the average school are as ɪ apart as the two poles. We are all familiar with the sta ment that the elementary curriculum is eminently adapt to produce clerks and accountants, but very poorly adapt to furnish recruits for any other department of life. T high school is criticized on the ground that it prepares : college and consequently for the professions, but that iɪ totally inadequate to the needs of the average citizen. N it would be futile to deny that there is some truth in bɛ these assertions, but I do not hesitate to affirm that both ɛ grossly exaggerated, and that the curriculum of today, w all its imperfections, does not justify so sweeping a denɪ ciation. I wish to point out some of the respects in whi these charges are fallacious, and, in so doing, perhaps, suggest some possible remedies for the defects that eveɪ one will acknowledge.

In the first place, let me make myself perfectly clear upon what I mean by the word "useful". What, after all, is the "useful" study in our schools? What do men find to be the useful thing in their lives? The most natural answer to this question is that the useful things are those that enable us to meet effectively the conditions of life,—or, to use a phrase that is perfectly clear to us all, the things that help us in getting a living. The vast majority of men and women in this world measure all value by this standard for most of us are, to use the expressive slang of the day, "up against" this problem, and "up against" it so hard and so constantly that we interpret everything in the greatly foreshortened perspective of immediate necessity. Most of us in this room are confronting this problem of making a living. At any rate, I am confronting it, and consequently I may lay claim to some of the authority that comes from experience.

And since I have made this personal reference, may I violate the canons of good taste and make still another? I was face to face with this problem of getting a living a good many years ago, when the opportunity came to me to take a college course. I could see nothing ahead after that except another tussle with this same vital issue. So I decided to take a college course which would, in all probability, help me to solve the problem. Scientific agriculture was not developed in those days as it has been since that time, but a start had been made, and the various agricultural colleges were offering what seemed to be very practical courses. I had had some early experience on the farm, and I decided to become a scientific farmer. I took the course of four years and secured my degree. The course was as useful from the standpoint of practical agriculture as any that could have been devised at the time. But when I graduated, what did I find? The same old problem of getting a living still confronted me as I had expected that it would; and alas! I had got my education in a profession that demanded capital. I was a landless farmer. Times were hard and work of all kinds was very scarce. The farmers of those days were in-

clined to scoff at scientific agriculture. I could have worked
for my board and a little more, and I should have done so had
I been able to find a job. But while I was looking for the
place, a chance came to teach school, and I took the opportunity as a means of keeping the wolf from the door. I have
been engaged in the work of teaching ever since. When I
was able to buy land, I did so, and I have today a farm of
which I am very proud. It does not pay large dividends, but I
keep it up for the fun I get out of it,—and I like to think,
also, that if I should lose my job as a teacher, I could go
back to the farm and show the natives how to make ·money.
This is doubtless an illusion, but it is a source of solid comfort just the same.

Now the point of this experience is simply this: I secured an education that seemed to me to promise the acme
of utility. In one way, it has fulfilled that promise far beyond my wildest expectations, but that way was very different from the one that I had anticipated. The technical
knowledge that I gained during those four strenuous years, I
apply now only as a means of recreation. So far as ena-
bling me directly to get a living, this technical knowledge
does not pay one per cent on the investment of time and
money. And yet, I count the training that I got from its
mastery as, perhaps, the most useful product of my education.

Now what was the secret of its utility? As I analyze
my experience, I find it summed up very largely in two factors. In the first place, I studied a set of subjects for which
I had at the outset very little taste. In studying agriculture, I had to master a certain amount of chemistry, physics,
botany, and zoology for each and every one of which I felt,
at the outset, a distinct aversion and dislike. A mastery of
these subjects was essential to a realization of the purpose
that I had in mind. I was sure that I should never like them,
and yet, as I kept at work, I gradually found myself losing
that initial distaste. First one and then another opened out
its vista of truth and revelation before me, and almost before

I was aware of it, I was an enthusiast over science. It was a long time before I generalized that experience and drew its lesson, but the lesson, once learned, has helped me more even in the specific task of getting a living than anything else that came out of my school training. That experience taught me, not only the necessity for doing disagreeable tasks,—for attacking them hopefully and cheerfully,—but it also taught me that disagreeable tasks, if attacked in the right way, and persisted in with patience, often become attractive in themselves. Over and over again in meeting the situations of real life, I have been confronted with tasks that were initially distasteful. Sometimes I have surrendered before them; but sometimes, too, that lesson has come back to me, and has inspired me to struggle on, and at no time has it disappointed me by the outcome. I repeat that there is no technical knowledge that I have gained that compares for a moment with that ideal of patience and persistence. When it comes to real, downright utility, measured by this inexorable standard of getting a living, commend me to the ideal of persistent effort. All the knowledge that we can learn or teach will come to very little if this element is lacking.

Now this is very far from saying that the pursuit of really useful knowledge may not give this ideal just as effectively as the pursuit of knowledge that will never be used. My point is simply this: that beyond the immediate utility of the *facts* that we teach,—basic and fundamental to this utility, in fact,—is the utility of the *ideals* and *standards* that are derived from our school work. Whatever we teach, these essential factors can be made to stand out in our work, and if our pupils acquire these we shall have done the basic and important thing in helping them to solve the problems of real life,—and if our pupils do not acquire these, it will make little difference how valuable may be the content of our instruction. I feel like emphasizing this matter today, because there is in the air a notion that utility depends entirely upon the content of the curriculum. Certainly the curriculum must be improved from this standpoint, but we are just now losing sight of the other equally important factor,—that, after all, while both are essential, it is the spirit of teaching rather than the content of teaching that is basic and fundamental.

Nor have I much sympathy with that extreme view of this matter which asserts that we must go out of our way to provide distasteful tasks for the pupil in order to develop this ideal of persistence. I believe that such a policy will always tend to defeat its own purpose. I know a teacher who holds this belief. He goes out of his way to make tasks difficult. He refuses to help pupils over hard places. He does not believe in careful assignments of lessons, because, he holds, the pupil ought to learn to overcome difficulties for himself and how can he learn unless real difficulties are presented?

The great trouble with this teacher is that his policy does not work out in practice. A small minority of his pupils are strengthened by it; the majority are weakened. He is right when he says that a pupil gains strength only by overcoming difficulties, but he neglects a very important qualification of this rule, namely, that a pupil gains no strength out of obstacles that he fails to overcome. It is the conquest that comes after effort,—this is the factor that gives one strength and confidence. But when defeat follows defeat and failure follows failure, it is weakness that is being engendered—not strength. And that is the trouble with this teacher's pupils. The majority leave him with all confidence in their own ability shaken out of them and some of them never recover from the experience.

And so while I insist strenuously that the most useful lesson we can teach our pupils is how to do disagreeable tasks cheerfully and willingly, please do not understand me to mean that we should go out of our way to provide disagreeable tasks. After all, I rejoice that my own children are learning how to read and write and cipher much more easily, much more quickly, and withal much more pleasantly than I learned those useful arts. The more quickly they get to the plane that their elders have reached, the more quickly they can get beyond this plane and on to the next level. To argue against improved methods in teaching on the ground that they make things too easy for the pupil is, to my mind, a grievous error. It is as fallacious as to argue that the introduction of machinery is a curse because it has diminished in some measure the necessity for human drudgery. But if machinery left mankind to rest upon its oars, if it discouraged further progress and further effortful achievement, it *would* be a curse: and if the easier and quicker methods of instruction simply bring my children to my own level and then fail to stimulate them to get beyond my level, then they are a curse and not a blessing. I do not decry that educational policy of today which insists that school work should be made as simple and attractive as possible. I do decry that misinterpretation of this policy which looks at the matter from the other side, and asserts so vehemently that the child should never be asked or urged to do something that isn't easy and attractive. Do I make myself clear upon this point? It is only because there is so much in the world to be done that, for the sake of economizing time and strength, we should raise the child as quickly and as rapidly and as pleasantly as possible to the plane that the race has reached. But among all the lessons of race-experience that we must teach him, there is none so fundamental and important as the lesson of achievement itself,—the supreme lesson wrung from human experience,—the lesson, namely, that every advance that the world has made, every step that it has taken forward, every increment that has been added to the sum-total of progress has been attained at the price of self-sacrifice and effort and struggle,—at the price of doing things that one does not want to do. And unless a man is willing to pay that price, he is bound to be the worst kind of a social parasite, for he is simply living on the experience of others, and adding to this capital nothing of his own.

It is sometimes said that universal education is essential in order that the great mass of humanity may live in greater comfort and enjoy the luxuries that in the past have been vouchsafed only to the few. Personally I think that this is all right so far as it goes, but it fails to reach an ultimate goal. Material comfort is justified only because it enables mankind to live more effectively on the lower planes of life and give greater strength and greater energy to the solution of new problems upon the higher planes of life. The end of life can never be adequately formulated in terms of comfort and ease, nor even in terms of culture and intellectual enjoyment; the end of life is achievement, and no matter how far we go, achievement is possible only to those who are willing to pay the price. When the race stops investing its capital of experience in further achievement, when it settles down to take life easy, it will not take it very long to eat up its capital and revert to the plane of the brute.

But I am getting away from my text. You will remember that I said that the most useful thing that we can teach the child is to attack strenuously and resolutely, any problem that confronts him whether it pleases him or not, and I wanted to be certain that you did not misinterpret me to mean that we should, for this reason, make our school tasks unnecessarily difficult and laborious. After all, while our attitude should always be one of interesting our pupils, their attitude should always be one of effortful attention,— of willingness to do the task that we think is best for them to do. You see it is a sort of a double-headed policy, and how to carry it out is a perplexing problem. Of so much I am certain, however, at the outset: if the pupil takes the attitude that we are there to interest and entertain him, we shall make a sorry fiasco of the whole matter, and inasmuch as this very tendency is in the air at the present time, I feel justified in at least referring to its danger.

Now if this ideal of persistent effort is the most useful thing that can come out of education, what is the next most useful? Again, as I analyze what I obtained from my own education, it seems to me that, next to learning that disagreeable tasks are often well worth doing, the factor that has helped me most in getting a living has been the *method* of solving the situations that confronted me. After all, if we simply have the ideal of resolute and agressive and persistent attack, we may struggle indefinitely without much result. All problems of life involve certain common factors. The essential difference between the educated and the uneducated man, if we grant each an equal measure of pluck, persistence, and endurance, lies in the superior ability of the educated man to analyze his problem effectively and to proceed intelligently rather than blindly to its solution. I maintain that education should give a man this ideal of attacking any problem; furthermore I maintain that the education of the present day, in spite of the anathemas that are hurled against it, is doing this in greater measure than it has ever been done before. But there is no reason why we should not do it in still greater measure.

I once knew two men who were in the busines of raising fruit for commercial purposes. Each had a large orchard which he operated according to conventional methods and which netted him a comfortable income. One of these men was a man of narrow education: the other a man of liberal education, although his training had not been directed in any way toward the problems of horticulture. The orchards had borne exceptionally well for several years, but one season, when the fruit looked especially promising, a period of wet, muggy weather came along just before the picking season, and one morning both these men went out into their orchards, to find the fruit very badly "specked." Now the conventional thing to do in such cases was well known to both men. Each had picked up a good deal of technical information about caring for fruit, and each did the same thing in meeting this situation. He got out his spraying outfit, prepared some Bordeaux mixture and set vigorously at work with his pumps. So far as persistence and enterprise went, both men stood on an equal footing. But it happened that this was an unusual and not a conventional situation. The spraying did not alleviate the condition. The corruption spread through the trees like wildfire and seemed to thrive on copper sulphate rather than succumb to its corrosive influence.

Now this was where the difference in training showed itself. The orchardist who worked by rule of thumb, when he found that his rule did not work, gave up the fight and spent his time sitting on his front porch cursing his luck. The other set diligently at work to analyze the situation. His education had not taught him anything about the characteristics of parasitic fungi, for parasitic fungi were not very well understood when he was in school. But his education had left with him a general method of procedure in just such cases, and that method he at once applied. It had taught him how to find the information that he needed, provided that such information was available. It had taught him that human experience is crystallized in books, and that, when a discovery is made in any field of science,—no matter how specialized the field and no matter how trivial the finding,—the discovery is recorded in printer's ink and placed at the disposal of those who have the intelligence to find it and apply it. And so he set out to read up on the subject,—to see what other men had learned about this peculiar kind of apple-rot. He got hold of all that had been written about it and began to master it. He told his friend about this material and suggested that the latter follow the same course, but the man of narrow education soon found himself utterly at sea in a maze of technical terms. The terms were new to the other too, but he took down his dictionary and worked them out. He knew how to use indices and tables of contents and various other devices that facilitate the gathering of information, and while his uneducated friend was storming over the pedantry of men who use big words, the other was making rapid progress through the material. In a short time he learned everything that had been found out about the specific disease. He learned that its spores are encased in a gelatinous sac which resisted the entrance of the chemicals. He found how the spores were reproduced, how they wintered, how they germinated in the following season; and, although he did not save much of his crop that year, he did better the next. Nor were the evidences of his superiority limited to this very useful result. He found that, after all, very little was known about this disease, so he set himself to find out more about it. To do this, he started where other investigators had left off, and then he applied a principle he had learned from his education,—namely, that the only valid methods of obtaining new truths are the methods of close observation and controlled experiment.

Now I maintain that the education which was given that man was effective in a degree that ought to make his experience an object-lesson for us who teach. What he had found most useful at a very critical juncture of his business life was, primarily, not the technical knowledge that he had gained either in school or in actual experience. His superiority lay in the fact that he knew how to get hold of knowledge when he needed it, how to master it once he had obtained it, how to apply it once he had mastered it, and finally how to go about to discover facts that had been undetected by previous investigators. I care not whether he got this knowledge in the elementary school or in the high school or in the college. He might have secured it in any one of the three types of institution but he had to learn it somewhere, and I shall go further and say that the average man has to learn it in some school and under an explicit and conscious method of instruction. That form of education which does not consciously teach pupils these four things will not supply a maximally useful form of information, I care not what the specific content is that it teaches. You cannot limit a useful *education* to what we call useful *information,* for information varies in its utility and we may load the pupil's mind with a mass of facts that he will never have occasion to apply. But if, in gaining these facts, he has acquired ideals of study and of investigation, I am willing to put him alongside the pupil who has been limited to facts that he does find useful, but who has missed the principles and ideals that I have mentioned.

But perhaps you would maintain that this statement of the case, while in general true, does not help us out in practice. After all, how are we to impress pupils with this ideal of persistence and with these ideals of getting and applying information, and with this ideal of investigation? I maintain that these important useful ideals can be effectively impressed from the very outset of school life. The teaching of every subject affords innumerable opportunities to force home their lessons. In fact, it must be a very gradual process—a process in which the concrete instances are numerous and rich and impressive. From these concrete instances, the general truth may in time emerge. Certainly the chances that it will emerge are greatly multiplied if we ourselves recognize its worth and importance, and lead pupils to see in each concrete case the operation of the general principle. After all, the chief reason why so much of our education miscarries, why so few pupils gain the strength and the power that we expect all to gain, lies in the inability of the average individual to draw a general conclusion from concrete cases—to see the general in the particular. We have insisted so strenuously upon concrete instruction that we have perhaps failed also to insist that fact without law is blind, and that observation without induction is stupidity gone to seed.

Let me give right here a concrete instance of what I mean. Not long ago, I visited an eighth-grade class during a geography period. It was at the time when the discovery of the Pole had just set the whole civilized world by the ears, and the teacher was doing something that many good teachers do on occasions of this sort: she was turning the vivid interest of the moment to educative purposes. The pupils had read Peary's account of his trip and they were discussing its details in class. Now that exercise was vastly more than an interesting information-lesson, for Peary's achievement became, under the skillful touch of that teacher, a type of all human achievement. I wish that I could reproduce that lesson for you—how vividly she pictured the situation that confronted the explorer,—the bitter cold, the shifting ice, the treacherous open leads, the lack of game or other sources of food-supply, the long marches on scant rations, the short hours and the uncomfortable conditions of sleep; and how from these that fundamental lesson of pluck and endurance and courage came forth naturally without preaching the moral or indulging in sentimental "goody-goodyism." And then the other and equally important part of the lesson, —how pluck and courage in themselves could never have solved the problem and how knowledge was essential, and how that knowledge had been gained: some of it from the experience of early explorers,—how to avoid the dreaded scurvy, how to build a ship that could withstand the tremendous pressure of the floes; and some from the Eskimos. —how to live in that barren region, and how to travel with dogs and sledges;—and some, too, from Peary's own early experiences,—how he had struggled for twenty years to reach the goal, and had added this experience to that until finally the prize was his. We may differ as to the value of Peary's deed but the fact that it stands as a type of what success in any undertaking means, no one can deny. And this was the lesson that these eighth-grade pupils were absorbing,—the world-old lesson before which all others fade into insignificance,—the lesson, namely, that achievement can be gained only by those who are willing to pay the price.

And I imagine that when that class is studying the continent of Africa in their geography work, they will learn something more than rivers and mountains and boundaries and products,—I imagine that they will link these facts with the names and deeds of the men who gave them to the world. And when they study history, it will be vastly more than a bare recital of dates and events,—it will be alive with these great lessons of struggle and triumph,—for history, after all, it is only the record of human achievement. And if those pupils do not find these same lessons coming out of their own little conquests,—if the problems of arithmetic do not furnish an opportunity to conquer the pressure-ridges of partial payments or the Polar-night of bank-discount, or if the intricacies of formal grammar do not resolve themselves into the North Pole of correct expression,—I have misjudged that teacher's capacities;—for, the great triumph of teaching is to get our pupils to see the fundamental and the eternal in things that are seemingly trivial and transitory. We are fond of dividing school studies into the cultural and the practical, into the humanities and the sciences. Believe me, there is no study worth the teaching that is not practical at basis, and there is no practical study that has not its human interest and its humanizing influence —if only we go to some pains to search them out.

I have said that the most useful thing that education can do is to imbue the pupil with the ideal of effortful achievement which will lead him to do cheerfully and effectively the disagreeable tasks that fall to his lot. I have said that the next most useful thing that it can do is to give him a general method of solving the problems that he meets. Is there any other useful out-come of a general nature that we can rank in importance with these two? I believe that there is, and I can perhaps tell you what I mean by another reference to a concrete case. I have a friend who lacks this third factor, although he possesses the other two in a very generous measuse. He is full of ambition, persistence, and courage. He is master of the rational method of solving the problems that beset him. He does his work intelligently and effectively. And yet he has failed to make a good living. Why? Simply because of his standard of what constitutes a good living. Measured by my standard, he is doing excellently well. Measured by his own standard, he is a miserable failure. He is depressed and gloomy and out of harmony with the world, simply because he has no other standard for a good living than a financial one. He is by profession a civil engineer. His work is much more remunerative than is that of many other callings. He has it in him to attain to professional distinction in that work. But to this opportunity he is blind. In the great industrial center in which he works, he is constantly irritated by the evidences of wealth and luxury beyond what he himself enjoys.   The millionaire captain-of-industry is his hero, and because he is not numbered among this class, he looks at the world through the bluest kind of spectacles.

Now, to my mind that man's education failed somewhere, and its failure lay in the fact that it did not develop in him ideals of success that would have made him immune to these irritating factors.   We have often heard it said that education should rid the mind of the incubus of superstition, and one very important effect of universal education is that it does offer to all men an explanation of the phenomena that formerly weighted down the mind with fear and dread, and opened an easy ingress to the forces of superstition and fraud and error.   Education has accomplished this function I think passably well with respect to the more obvious sources of superstition.   Necromancy and magic, demonism and witchcraft have long since been relegated to the limbo of exposed fraud.   Their conquest has been one of the most significant advances that man has made above the brute.   The truths of science have at last triumphed, and, as education has diffused these truths among the masses, the triumph has become almost universal.   But there are other forms of superstition beside those I have mentioned,—other instances of a false perspective, of distorted values, of inadequate standards.   If belief in witchcraft or in magic is bad because it falls short of an adequate interpretation of nature,—if it is false because it is inconsistent with human experience,—then the worship of Mammon that my engineer-friend represents is tenfold worse than witchcraft, measured by the same standards.   If there is any lesson that human history teaches with compelling force it is surely this: Every race which has yielded to the demon of individualism and the lust for gold and self-gratification has gone down the swift and certain road to national decay.   Every race that, through unusual material prosperity, has lost its grip on the eternal verities of self-sacrifice and self-abnegation has left the lesson of its downfall written large upon the pages of history.   I repeat that if superstition consists in believing something that is inconsistent with rational

human experience, then our present worship of the golden
calf isby far the most dangerous form of superstition that has
ever befuddled the human intellect.

But, you ask, what can education do in alleviating a
condition of this sort? How can the weak influence of the
school make itself felt in an environment that has crystallized on every hand this unfortunate standard? Individualism is in the air. It is the dominant spirit of the times. It
is reinforced upon every side by the unmistakable evidences
of national prosperity. It is all right to preach the simple
life, but who is going to live it unless he has to? It is all
right to say that man should have social and not individual
standards of success and achievement, but what effect will
your puerile assertion have upon the situation that confronts us?

Yes; it is easier to be a pessimist than an optimist. It
is far easier to lie back and let things run their course than it
is to strike out into mid-stream and make what must be for
the pioneer a fatal effort to stem the current. But is the situation absolutely hopeless? If the forces of education can lift
the Japanese people from barbarism to enlightenment in two
generations;—if education can in a single century transform
Germany from the weakest to the strongest power on the
continent of Europe;—if five short years of a certain type
of education can change the course of destiny in China; are
we warranted in our assumption that we hold a weak weapon
in this fight against Mammon?

I have intimated that the attitude of my engineer-friend
toward life is the result of twisted ideals. A good many
young men, are going out into life with a similar defect in
their education. They gain their ideals, not from the great
well-springs of human experience as represented in history
and literature, in religion and art, but from the environment
around them, and consequently they become victims of this
superstition from the outset. As a trainer of teachers, I
hold it to be one important part of my duty to fortify my
students as strongly as I can against this false standard of

which my engineer-friend is the victim. It is just as much a part of my duty to give my students effective and consistent standards of what a good living consists in as it is to give them the technical knowledge and skill that will enable them to make a good living. If my students who are to become teachers have standards of living and standards of success that are inconsistent with the great ideal of social service for which teaching stands, then I have fallen far short of success in my work. If they are constantly irritated by the evidences of luxury beyond their means, if this irritation sours their dispositions and checks their spontaneity, their efficiency as teachers is greatly lessened or perhaps entirely negated. And if my engineer-friend places worldly emoluments upon a higher plane than professional efficiency, I dread for the safety of the bridges that he builds. His education as an engineer should have fortified him against just such a contingency. It should have left him with the ideal of craftmanship supreme in his life. And if his technical education failed to do this, his general education ought, at least, to have given him a bias in the right direction.

I believe that all forms of vocational and professional education are not so strong in this respect as they should be. Again you say to me, What can education do when the spirit of the times speaks so strongly on the other side? But what is education for if it is not to preserve midst the chaos and confusion of troublous times the great truths that the race has wrung from its experience? How different might have been the fate of Rome, if Rome had possessed an educational system touching every child in the Empire, and if, during the years that witnessed her decay and downfall, those schools could have kept steadily, persistently at work, impressing upon every member of each successive generation the virtues that had made the old Romans strong and virile, —the virtues that enabled them to lay the foundations of an Empire that crumbled in ruins once these truths were forgotten. Is it not the specific task of education to represent in each generation the human experiences that have been

tried and tested and found to work,—to represent these in
the face of opposition if need be,—to be faithful to the trus-
teeship of the most priceless legacy that the past has left to
the present and to the future? If this is not our function in
the scheme of things, then what is our function? Is it to
stand with bated breath to catch the first whisper that will
usher in the next change? Is it to surrender all initiative
and simply allow ourselves to be tossed hither and yon by
the waves and cross-waves of a fickle public opinion? Is it
to cower in dread of a criticism that is not only unjust, but
also ill-advised of the real conditions under which we are
doing our work?

I take it that none of us is ready to answer these
questions in the affirmative. Deep down in our hearts
we know that we have a useful work to do, and we know
that we are doing it passably well. We also know our
defects and shortcomings at least as well as one who has
never faced our problems and tried to solve them. And it
is from this latter type that most of the drastic criticism,
especially of the elementary and secondary school, emanates.
I confess that my gorge rises within me when I read or hear
the invectives that are being hurled against teaching as a
profession (and against the work of the elementary and secondary school in particular) by men who know nothing of
this work at first hand. This is the greatest handicap under
which the profession of teaching labors. In every other important field of human activity a man must present his cre-
dentials before he takes his seat at the council-table, and
even then he must sit and listen respectfully to his elders
for a while before he ventures a criticism or even a sugges-
tion. This plan may have its defects. It may keep things
on too conservative a basis; but it avoids the danger into
which we as a profession have fallen,—the danger of "half-
baked" theories and unmatured policies. Today the only
man that can get a respectable hearing at our great national
educational meetings is the man who has something new and
bizarre to propose. And the more startling the proposal,

the greater the measure of adulation that he receives. The result of this is a continual straining for effect, an enormous annual crop of fads and fancies, which, though most of them are happily short-lived, keep us in a state of continual turmoil and confusion.

Now it goes without saying that there are many ways of making education hit the mark of utility in addition to those that I have mentioned. The teachers down in the lower grades who are teaching little children the arts of reading and writing and computation are doing vastly more in a practical direction than they are ever given credit for doing; for reading and writing and the manipulation of numbers are, next to oral speech itself, the prime necessities in the social and industrial world. These arts are being taught today better than they have ever been taught before,—and the method and technique of their teaching is undergoing constant refinement and improvement.

The school can do and is doing other useful things. Some schools are training their pupils to be well mannered and courteous and considerate of the rights of others. They are teaching children one of the most basic and fundamental laws of human life,—namely, that there are some things that a gentleman cannot do and some things that society will not stand. How many a painful experience in solving that very problem of getting a living could be avoided if one had only learned this lesson passing well! What a pity it is that some schools that stand today for what we call educational progress are failing in just this particular— are sending out into the world an annual crop of boys and girls who must learn the great lesson of self-control and a proper respect for the rights of others in the bitter school of experience,—a school in which the rod will never be spared, but whose chastening scourge comes sometimes alas too late!

Yes, there is no feature of school life which has not its almost infinite possibilities of utility. But after all, are not the basic and fundamental things these ideals that I have named?   And should not we who teach stand for idealism in its widest sense?   Should we not insist, in court and out, that this nation of ours was founded upon idealism, and that, whatever may be the materialistic and individualistic tendencies of the moment, its children, at least, shall learn to dwell among the sunlit peaks?   And should we not ourselves subscribe an undying fidelity to those great ideals for which teaching must stand,—to the ideal of social service which lies at the basis of our craft, to the ideals of effort and discipline that make a nation great and its children strong, to the ideal of science that dissipates the black night of ignorance and superstition, to the ideal of culture that humanizes mankind?   For if we have these great human truths well implanted, although our work may keep us very close to Mother Earth, we can still lift our heads above the fog and look the morning sun squarely in the face.

UNIVERSITY OF ILLINOIS

PRESIDENT'S OFFICE

SCHOOL BULLETIN

DECEMBER 1, 1910.

READING IN THE GRADES

SECOND EDITION

BY

KATHARINE GILL

Normal School Bulletin

PUBLISHED BY THE EASTERN ILLINOIS STATE NORMAL SCHOOL

Entered March 5, 1902, as second-class matter, at the Post office at Charleston, Illinois, Act of Congress, July 16, 1894.

CHARLESTON, ILLINOIS, DECEMBER 1, 1910   No. 30.

RE_A_DING IN THE GR_A_DES

SECOND EDITION

By K_A_TH_A_RINE GILL,

Instructor in Reading

T HE subject of reading is far too broad and many-sided to admit of anything like full treatment in a single paper. It can be stretched to embrace everything from simple sight reading up through the recital of dramatic monologues to the presentation of a play; and at each step we should find material for extended discussion. The purpose of this paper, however, limits it to the consideration of the teaching of oral reading, or the expression of the thoughts of others, in the grades, and this purpose must include a careful study of the material to be used to accomplish certain results. It must be kept in mind that the term reading as used here means oral reading only; it does not include the study of literature or language, except as such study is inevitable in learning to read aloud intelligently and effectively. To the writer, moreover, an oral reading lesson means something very definite. It means a lively, interesting recitation in which some good bit of literature is used for a definite purpose. It means every-day work with the pupil for rounded development in expression.

The idea of correlation has been so overdone, so abused, that one may seriously question the wisdom of its application to oral reading. The subject of reading is so many times made to correlate with other subjects that the child, and I doubt not the teacher also, becomes bewildered and hardly knows what he is studying. For his most rapid advancement, it is well to have it clearly understood that the end and aim of all work in the reading class is oral reading—good, intelligent, appreciative, enjoyable reading aloud of literature which, because of the beauty or energy of its thought and language, is worth reading aloud; that an oral reading lesson should not be a language lesson, save as one learns language by reading, committing, and reciting from the best authors; and that it should not be a literature lesson, except as the study for thought and for the expression of the thought is one form of the study of literature. Neither should an oral reading lesson be a lesson in physiology, to use an absurd illustration, just because a broken arm or leg is spoken of in the selection studied.

True, a reading lesson may be a mere reading lesson, and at the same time be, indirectly, a valuable lesson in history or biography, or may yet contribute to the pupil's knowledge of the natural world. A varied course in reading might include some vivid chapters from the historian or biographer or a bit from the best work of some great naturalist; but the teacher should keep in mind that any such selection is given the pupil for the sake of helping him to express the author's thought, and not for the sake of teaching him the number of facts it may present, or of correlating with something else the information contained therein. Lastly, a lesson in oral reading should not be an exercise in lecturing on the part of the teacher or of conversation with the children.   It should be first and always one thing; at all times the emphasis should be laid on the oral expression.   This motive should dominate the lesson.   If other results than these definitely worked for creep in, well and good.   Other results than good oral reading there certainly will be, but they are not to be worked for, lest the primary object be weakened, or, as in so many cases, lost sight of entirely.   Steady work along one line at a time brings better results than the diffusive scattering over several lines, as is sometimes seen.   The straight and narrow path in the study of reading brings early rewards, as concentration always does.

In addition to concentration of purpose during the recitation, the oral reading lesson should have its own period of time each day.   This hour, even if it must be a short one, should be set aside every day, in every grade and—let it be said most emphatically—of this hour not one minute should be given to spelling, word analysis, language lessons, history, literature, or any other subject.

In the recitation, the important work of thought-getting, of seeing, understanding, realizing, and feeling must come first.   There are always certain points that must be explained and cleared up; a particular setting is often required and an atmosphere for the selection studied must be created.   The children must be put in harmony with the story, poem, or oration itself.   All of this may be done little at a time, as the recitation progresses, and the work of oral reading may move along throughout the entire hour.   The recitation hour is one of effort, of continuous, repeated effort,—of effort to help the pupils get the thought of what they are reading; of effort to make them see, understand, feel; finally, of effort to help them to express orally what they see, understand, and feel.   When the hour is over, every member of the class should have had the privilege of expressing, in his best manner, some one or two thoughts, at least, and not only the teacher, but the pupils themselves, should feel that they have gained in the art of expressing.

Occasionally, an important part of the lesson is the assignment.   Some of the interest of tomorrow's work depends upon what is said today about the new lesson.   In this, methods will vary as much as in the presentation of the subject, but for many, perhaps, the following suggestions will be helpful. In all grades, even in the higher ones, knowledge of words is so meagre that it seems best to say when assigning a new piece: "Read the lesson through aloud to find out what it is about.   If you do not know at the end of the first reading, read it until you do know.   Then, when you know what it is about, read it again.   If it is a story, in this reading, watch the people, the characters.   Try to see them move, listen to their voices, study their faces, see how they treat each other.   Feel that you are looking at a play. Notice the action, the settings for the action, and the like.   If the lesson to be studied is any bit of description, either prose or poetry, look at the little pictures that come to you as you read. Try to feel that you are on a train.   As you go forward, pictures flash by you.   There is a pretty bit of woods, a river, a bridge, a winding road, a cornfield, broad meadows with hills beyond; you catch glimpses of the sky—now a deep blue, now barred or flecked with clouds.   Maybe you are running right into a sunset.   As you read let the pictures go by you in the same way.   Each one will leave its impress upon your mind, so that when you get through, you have a larger picture of the whole.   Now read your lesson once more as if you were reading it to an audience.   Try to feel that a number of people must hear and understand every word you utter, and see every bit of action or description that you give. If you are reading a part of an oration, try to im-press the author's purpose—which, for the time being, is your own—upon your imaginary audience."

These are a few of the points which, from time to time, one might make in assigning lessons. Each lesson demands its own peculiar suggestions. All of this is with the idea of securing pleasant study. Another and equally important way of getting satisfactory study is to use tact, care, and taste in the selection of the matter to be studied. This brings us to the discussion of the material that is used in oral read-ing classes.

Just at present there is a strong feeling in favor of the use of the complete classics, however long they may be. Works of the class of Evangeline, Hiawatha, The Lady of the Lake, A Christmas Carol, Silas Marner, Water Babies, The Last of the Mohicans are used. They are read in class, discussed, and recited upon little at a time. Weeks and often months are spent upon this study of a single selection. Those that advocate this method of teaching reading do so strongly, and some of the reasons they give are the following:

1.   That when through with the study of a certain classic upon which months have been spent, the pupils have it for life. They have its background, its whole setting, its thought, its story, its style, its purpose, moral, intellectual, or aesthetic.

2.   That a stronger interest is developed by the study of the same thing for a number of weeks, and that the interest grows as the pupils progress.

3.   That a much deeper insight into the author's meaning and purpose is secured by this long study of one selection.

4.   That the moral effect of a complete masterpiece is deeper and more permanent; that the characters acting in different situations reveal the author's motives; and that the thread of his thought is shown in a steady sequence.

5.   That a complete masterpiece studied as a whole shows the author's power.

6.   That a classic is often a picture of an age, a panoramic survey of an historical epoch; and that the only way to get the complete picture is to study the whole.

Now for the answers to these points:

1.   All those that make use of the long classics, with the above purpose in mind in the teaching of oral reading, are confusing two subjects, Literature and Oral Reading—subjects which, in their teaching, ought to be kept far apart. The study of oral reading is one thing; that of literature, another. In one sense, we all agree that they are one subject.   There can be no practice of oral reading without literature; no study of literature without reading.   But the training required for growth in these two subjects is, or should be, essentially different.   In the class in literature, we aim at the largest appropriation of the great thoughts and feelings of our race; in the oral reading class, we are seeking the exercise of the pupil's individual power to express such of these thoughts as he is capable of making vitally his own.   One purpose or set of purposes should dominate in the teaching of oral reading; another set of purposes must dominate in the teaching of literature.   These purposes carried out bring the subjects together in time.   Before that time, there should be a long period when they should be kept distinctly apart.   The reasons for this are not far to seek.

2.   Probably all teachers acknowledge that growth in any study depends to a greater or less extent upon the interest taken in that subject.   In the study of reading, however, growth to the greatest extent depends upon interest. There is little danger of making too much of this point. There are just as many individualities in the class as there are pupils, and the study of these individualities is the teach-

er's work. Each individual mind has its own peculiar needs, and the teacher of reading, as much as any other, must make a study of these needs and adapt the work to them. She must find out what will aid most in the growth, what will interest most, and then supply the material accordingly. It does not seem reasonable to say that any one poem or story or oration can give the matter needed to arouse and keep alive the absorbing interest of a large number of children— an interest strong enough to produce growth; and I do not now recall the classic that can furnish the great variety essential to the development of the diversity of minds and characters found to be in every class.

I believe that the dreary droning over of a classic, day after day for weeks and months, certainly kills the pupil's interest in the classic. If such a work as Evangeline, for instance, were studied as it should be in oral reading, it would be divided into parts. Each part would be taken to pieces, drilled on, and worked over from a number of points of view. There would be the necessary painstaking care of the articulation; the needed repetitions of hard words; the urgent call for getting the thoughts, pictures, and situations; the committing of the best lines; the oral expression; the dramatic readings—and so on indefinitely. By the time this work, which must cover from two to three months, is done, what is left of Evangeline as a poem? All poetry, romance, and deliciousness have been sacrificed to drill work. Reverence for the thing itself is gone. Undue familiarity, too intimate an acquaintance has dispelled its charm and made it all common. Everything is known. Nothing is left to the fancy or imagination. Poetry and romance have become prosaic platitudes. Violets and roses have become dry and expressionless.

Instead of this long weary study, which must tire the teacher as much as the pupil, why not take a vivid, interesting passage from this poem? Give it its proper setting by a lively review of the story; illuminate it; throw a glamour of romance about it; arouse expectancy; then, with the class in sympathy, read it orally for all there is in it. Then drop it. I feel sure that the interest aroused by such study will be lasting enough to send the pupil to the poem itself, to make him read the whole for his own pleasure. Then in his reading, there will be no tiring work on detail. Instead, he will be absorbed in the main lines of the plot, the play of the characters, and the march of events; and unconsciously he will read into the whole the illuminating points given by the teacher in the study of the part. In the meantime, in the class, work has moved on to other things. There will be study on a beautiful poem today, some powerful lines from an oration tomorrow, a story the next day, and so on; and interest will grow from day to day as the outlook broadens.

3. As to securing a deeper insight into the author's meaning and purpose by long study, there can be no doubt. It certainly should be so. But what of it? Will not the student get this insight in his regular study of literature when the time comes for it? And will this insight into the purpose and power of one author in one selection help the student in his oral expression in general? Will it give him versatility? Will it give him power to adapt himself readily to different styles? Is it all important that a pupil be saturated with the style, diction, and rhythm of Miles Standish, we will say, to the exclusion, for the time being, of all other forms of literature? Will he not grow faster if he is made to struggle with forms that require different kinds of effort or purpose? The purpose of the orator is perhaps to make people think and act along a definite line. Although he may excite the imagination and play upon the emotions, he all the while is trying

to dominate the will. The poet is almost exclusively absorbed with the aesthetic and his effects are produced through appeals to the imagination and feelings. The story-teller asks for sympathy for and with his characters as they move before the eye of the reader; he deals with human motives, passions, and purposes; he interprets human nature. The essayist makes demands upon the judgment and reasoning powers. The reader is asked to think, to analyze, to weigh and consider. These are a few of the many varieties of literature that may be placed before oral reading classes. Will not the pupil who is helped to express himself through the medium of these different styles, to interpret these diverse thoughts, emotions, and purposes, grow faster in expressiveness, in adaptability to the new, in versatility, in insight, than the one who is kept for weeks upon a work that reveals the style, diction, purpose, and power of one man in one production?

4. It may be, also, as has been contended, that the moral effect of a complete masterpiece is deeper and more permanent, but what after all is meant by the moral effect? Does it mean getting the point of a sermon, the text, the underlying thought? Or does it mean the growing realization of what is charming, beautiful, exquisite, noble? Does it not mean intellectual growth, a response to the aesthetic in the work studied, a quickened pulse, a thrill of delight at a happy turning of a phase of thought, the quick grasp of a startling situation, or the discovery of a new character? Whatever it means, there is no doubt that it may be cultivated more quickly through coming in contact with a variety of material than through long study on a single work.

5—6. All of the other points given to prove that the use of the long selection is better adapted to oral reading than the short—as, that one gets the author's thought more fully in a steady sequence, that a classic is often a picture of an age, and so on—must be passed over. The experienced teacher knows that much of this is gained through the study of the short selection, not so fully, to be sure, as through effort upon an entire work,—but why should it be? All of this kind of culture comes to the student of literature proper. The problem of the reading teacher is a very different one. She is making an effort to help her children gain: First, in smoothness of articulation and enunciation; second, in the use of the voice; third, in the training of the eye and ear; fourth, in sensing thoughts; fifth, in expressing thoughts; sixth, in growth in freedom; seventh; in cultivating in general a taste for reading and for good literature.

A way of bringing all of this about is to place before the pupil the very best that literature offers. The choice must be as varied as his needs, or as the needs of the class. One pupil in a class can grasp the thought of an oration, but he sees nothing in poetry. A poem, to him, is merely a composition made up of long and short lines, every one of which begins with a capital letter. The sentiment that could inspire "Hark! hark! the lark!" or "I wandered lonely as a cloud," he knows nothing about. For his own sake, he must be taught to recognize these elements of beauty when he sees them. Another boy may quickly enjoy and grasp the action of the characters in a story. He may have a dramatic instinct for the movements and motives of people. He is entirely unable to see any of the deep purpose in some essay or oration. If he does not study the heavier forms of literature and get a background for his dramatic taste, the dramatic instinct is sure to lead him to things cheap and common. One pupil needs help along one line, another needs something different.

The teacher does the most good to the greatest number by giving variety in subject-matter to her classes in oral reading.

The rollicking Blind Man's Buff sketch will enliven all.   The quickly responsive will enjoy it fully, the unresponsive will be helped by making the effort to enjoy.   The whole class, tomorrow, will examine "The Blue Gentian" and find undreamed of beauty there.   Next week, Mr. Pickwick and his inimitable coterie will arouse a surprising enthusiasm. Some other day, the life and action in "How They Brought the Good News From Ghent to Aix" will thrill the class.   And so on indefinitely.

There is no doubt to my mind that the art side of this subject can be more readily reached through the use of the short selection, not only art in teaching, in the instilling of artistic purpose and feeling, but art in the expressing of purpose and feeling.   Along with this there is less danger of the mechanical side's being made too much of.   All teachers know the evils that arise from the use of mechanics, evils that deceive by seeming to secure results quickly.   Among other things, the use of mechanics produces what is sometimes a great evil, imitation,—imitation that results in a decided narrowing and confining of powers, imitation that interferes with the growth of power to originate and create, imitation that produces superficiality and that kills all spontaneity in expression. One of the beauties of oral reading or expression is the spontaneous response of the whole nature to the thought, the quick feeling that changes as the thought changes, the expression of the face and the color of the voice, which grow out of the play of the imagination;—all this and more belongs to the art of expression.   The use of mechanics in this art is withering in its effect.

In this study, there must be progression in development, and this progression absolutely demands variety of literature. Growth begins at a certain point and goes on from there.   It moves from the plane of the common to the uncommon, from

the real to the ideal, from the ideal to the suggestive. A
simple example will in part illustrate this growth. Some
pupils, no matter what their age or condition, see little on a
page but words. Take one of this class, one that can pro-
nounce words moderately well. The highest emotion this
pupil is able to express at first, perhaps', is the coarse anger,
the petty rage of a Mrs. Caudle. If he has the saving grace
of a sense of humor, he may be able to respond to the broad
fun some of the people of Dickens. After a large response
of this kind to characters and scenes of a certain type, it will
be found that in the study of a poem, pictures will form themselves more quickly. Little by little his taste takes him
away from the coarse and bald to the beautiful or heroic in
the world of man and nature about him. Before long he will
be feeling and expressing some of the joy that the poets felt
when they wrote their most perfect lyrics. It is not too much
to say that he will really appreciate the delicate delight of
the dancing daffodils, that the flight of the skylark as it
"melts into the pale purple even" will be something more
than the mere flying away of a bird. Not only the pictures
of such poems, but the sentiments that called them into being, the subjective processes that underlie them, in a
measure he will feel and appreciate.

This same evolution may be seen in character study. For
example, when our pupils take up any part of a play, we will
say The Merchant of Venice, the only emotion that can be
aroused, in fact the only emotion that can be asked for at
first, in the study of Shylock, is one of a very low order. A
very small part of the personal, impotent rage and anger of
Shylock towards Antonio and his class is all that can be ex-
pressed. Gradually, by appeals to something higher in
their natures, the feeling that they give to Shylock rises to a
higher plane. As they study the life of this man, and see

what his sufferings were, through his own inherited tendencies and those of his natural enemies, the Christians; when
they look upon him, and see instead of the traditional Jew,
an old man with the whole world, including his only child,
against him; when, in short, they begin to realize that he is
flesh and blood, sympathy takes the place of scorn.   A look
of pity replaces the smile which in early study of this character usually comes at the revilings of Antonio and his friends;
and as realization grows, a nobler emotion arouses a finer
response in the reader than the first, which found expression
in ranting and raving.   This response affects the face, the
voice, the whole body because it is aroused from within, because it is the expression of a real, a living sympathy for this
man and his race.

Let us take one speech of Shylock's to illustrate.   It is
that long speech in which he sums up his personal wrongs
and those of his whole tribe.   One morning Shylock was
walking along a street in Venice, busy with his thoughts,
which were bitter enough just then. Jessica, his daughter, had
eloped with a Christian and, moreover, had taken with her
money and jewels belonging to her father.   Shylock did not
come out upon the street to tell the story of his additional
sorrow to anyone; but, he is met by two young fellows,
friends of Antonio's. These creatures buzz around him, sting
him, and irritate him to such a degree that he finally turns
upon them, and in the anger, rage, and heat of the moment,
delivers this tremendous speech. Now, in our reading classes,
when we take this scene up for the first time, the pupils jum-
ble the parts together. You remember that Shylock says,
"He hath disgraced me and hindered me half a million, laugh-
ed at my losses, mocked at my gains, scorned my nation,
thwarted my bargains, cooled my friends, heated mine enemies, and what's his reason? I am a Jew" The pupil at

first does not differentiate these wrongs. To him they are all alike. He does not realize what "scorned my nation" means to Shylock. "Thwarted my bargains, cooled my friends, heated mine enemies" mean no more to this pupil, in an early reading, than "John spilled my ink" would mean—not so much in some cases. And so he reads these statements just as he conceives them.

The reading is dull and colorless. There is no depth in the thought, no slide in the voice, nothing that would indicate shades of thought. But when he realizes that each one of these statements comes from a deep underlying sense of wrong, that the wrongs are as numerous and as various as the statements themselves, after he reflects upon the life of Shylock, upon the position he holds in the social and business world, then color comes to the voice, action comes to the body, in fact expression is given to these thoughts. You see he has something within to express. His work is lifted from the plane of the very realistic, perhaps not to the suggestive—only rarely do we reach that plane,—but at least toward the ideal.

This pupil is discovering truth. And now when he is nearing the ideal, on his way to the suggestive, turn him to the breadth and majesty of the book of Kings, of Isaiah, of Job, to the beauty of the Gospel narratives, to the exquisite imaginative play of fancy of the Revelations, to the adoration and exaltation of the Psalms. One difficulty that stands in the way of bringing these selections into the reading class, is a feeling that the thoughts and emotions are too high, that the average pupil cannot attain to anything like an adequate expression of such sentiments, and yet in the whole field of literature, there is none that sets forth so wide a range of human experience as these and similar productions. The problem is the point of contact and the case is not essentially different from that of Shylock's speech. In grasping the emotions of Shylock, the pupil began with the kind of petty indignation of which he himself was capable, and grew to a realization of just and righteous anger. So in reading this magnificent literature, the expression might have the same personal narrowness. The pupil's own power of love and gratitude would at first set the limits of his expression of David's praise and adoration; but a growing sense of the occasion, the depth of David's feeling, and the world-wide meaning of a great psalm would gradually break down the barriers and open the way to a fuller and deeper emotional content.

The expression of such content is the reflection of the inner-man, of much of his life; and there can be no expression of the noble, the majestic, the beautiful, no realization of the fanciful, no belief in that which is suggested by the miracle— there can be no such expression unless there are in the reader elements, at least, of nobility, beauty, majesty, breadth of thought. The cultivation of all this is where the art side of the teaching of reading is shown. Grateful results are early apparent, not only in upper grades, but in all grades where reading is taught. And of these results, a few are—versatility, a readiness, an alertness of both body and mind, to say nothing of actual growth in character.

To sum up briefly:

First. Oral reading as a subject in the grades should be a part of every school programme every day.

Second. As oral reading is to accomplish a certain end, and as there are too few real classics to admit of the spoiling of even one, the study of the long classics should be left to the teacher of literature.

Third. As all elements necessary for the growth of the student of expression are not to be found in a single story or poem or oration, the teacher gives the most good to the greatest number by using, in oral reading classes, a large variety of short selections.

Fourth. Oral reading should be approached more from the art side. It should be made, not a means for the gleaning of facts or the advancement of pedagogical methods, but a medium for the best expression of the best thoughts and feeling from the best books.

OCTOBER 1, 1912.

ARGUMENTS FOR VOCATIONAL GUIDANCE

BY

E. E. LEWIS.

Normal School Bulletin

PUBLISHED BY THE EASTERN ILLINOIS STATE NORMAL SCHOOL

Entered March 5, 1902, as second-class matter, at the Post office at Charleston, Illinois, Act of Congress, July 16, 1894.

CHARLESTON, ILLINOIS, OCTOBER 1, 1912   No. 38.

ARGUMENTS FOR VOCATIONAL GUIDANCE

Pointing out how the gap between school life and vocational
life may be bridged in part by the
public school teacher.

"No two persons are born alike, but each differs from the other in individual endowments, one being suited for one thing, and another for another; and all things will be provided in superior quantity and quality, and with greater ease, when each man works at a single occupation, in accordance with his natural gifts."

—Plato, Republic, Book II.

The Relation of Vocational Guidance to Education.

The majority of our boys and girls at fourteen, fifteen and sixteen are becoming independent wage-earners;—How can they best be guided and safe-guarded during their earlier years of labor and the perilous years of adolescence? This is the question that is being asked almost universally, and to which education is gradually giving heed. Realizing the helplessness of the child, and his inability, by reason of youth and inexperience, to protect himself as an independent worker in the complex industries of today, an enlightened public opinion is bringing about a change in the aim, methods and materials of education that is gratifying to all those who are interested in raising the standards of citizenship and in increasing the efficiency of workers. Out of the social consciousness have grown agencies, both public and private in character, devoted to the cause of extending the period of childhood, and of protecting by all possible means the period of adolescence and plasticity. In no uncertain language society has set its stamp of disapproval upon the unregulated employment of immature citizens. Legislation the world over has built up barriers in the interest of future populations, driving children out of the homes and streets, out of the shops, stores and trades into the healthier atmosphere of the schoolroom. Civic organizations, social workers, labor unions, political parties, educational authorities and all kindred groups have united in a vigorous campaign for the elimination of un-educative and health-breaking forms of child labor.

Gradually the conception has grown that laws alone are inadequate to combat this evil unless supplemented by a series of educational institutions that more directly meet the varying needs of young workers. The cry is for an education of "all the children of all the people"; "a universal education, free and equally open to all and suited to the needs of each." The one adequate remedy for child labor, upon which all people seemingly are beginning to agree, is to be found in a public system of vocational education that provides for and protects young workers in all lines until they are at least 18 years old.

The old apprenticeship system of training the young worker in the home and under the personal direction of the master mechanic, and the guild to which he belonged, has proved incompetent. The introduction of machinery has substituted unskilled for skilled labor in so many industries that a compulsory apprenticeship permits the employer too great an opportunity to exploit the health and labor of the child for his own capitalistic ends. Nor is there longer any security to the public that the apprentice will be thoroughly and efficiently taught. Again, the apprenticeship system has in the past, and must in the future, leave outside of its scope a large proportion of children who are not able to get into skilled lines in which alone apprenticeship is possible. And lastly, the apprenticeship system has always been confined to a few fields of organized labor, and the public, wisely, or unwisely, fear that it will be used as a device to maintain a monopoly.

The enactment of Child Labor and Compulsory Attendance Laws are merely negative checks to the evils of uneducative juvenile employment. By the passage of such laws the state acknowledges both its right and its duty concerning the education and labor of juveniles. Such laws are very beneficial in almost entirely keeping children out of work until they are 12 and 14 years old, and in rigidly prescribing the conditions under which they may labor until they are 16. The factory inspectors and attendance officers have, in the enforcement of their duties, incidentally done a great deal in keeping many children in school, and in placing others in suitable occupations when schooling was impossible. It was never intended that laws and officers of this character should assume the entire burden of training and supervising juveniles during their earlier vocational experiences. These measures are coercive rather than educative, negative rather than positive. They delay and check but do not solve the evils of child labor. More positive remedies are needed.

It is not enough to keep children out of work and in school. Raising the school-leaving age works a hardship upon many children, if, at the same time, the school does not provide some form of industrial and vocational training for the great percentage of children who later enter industrial occupations. All economists, educational experts and social workers, who have been brought into intimate touch with modern problems, are agreed upon the relation of misemployment to adolescence, and regard an improved and extended educational system as an urgent necessity.

Now, education is definable in a thousand and one ways. We are all familiar with, and tired of most of these definitions. Vocational education should not be confused with liberal or cultural education on the one hand, nor with industrial education on the other. It is neither of these. True, the educational process is a unity in the life of an individual. Yet, there are convenient divisions within that process. One part may be called liberal, another industrial, and a third vocational. Or, the total process may be called liberal, or industrial, or vocational.

Dean Russell, of Teachers College, has pointed out three kinds of knowledge with which the school deals, or with which it should deal. The first he calls humanistic, the second scientific, and the third industrial. He argues that the school has thus far concerned itself almost exclusively with humanistic knowledge, very slightly in the last few years with scientific knowledge, and as yet scarcely at all with industrial knowledge. The schooling that deals largely with the first two types of knowledge we are in the habit of calling liberal and cultural. The schooling that deals with industrial knowledge we are beginning to call industrial. Of late the importance of this third kind of knowledge has been repeatedly urged and throughout the world there has arisen a movement to promote the introduction of industrial knowledge or subject matter in the school curriculum alongside of, and in intimate connection with, liberal and scientific subject matter. This movement is known as the Industrial Education Movement.

Here, then, we have two distinguishable steps in the educational process. We want our children to learn something about the subjects, which in an old-fashioned way, are styled the sciences and the humanities, and, at the same time, we want our children to learn something about the tremendous and marvelous industries that have grown up in the last few decades. If it is one of the functions of education to easily and quickly pass on knowledge from one generation to the next, we are beginning to wonder if this great mass of industrial knowledge that has been so rapidly acquired does not need to be passed on to the next generation in order to be preserved as well as the older knowledge which the race has accumulated in the past centuries. This is the fundamental idea underneath the movement for the promotion of industrial education. The aim of industrial education is, then, to introduce industrial subject matter into the curricula of the various schools. This means all schools from the kindergarten to the university. The aim of liberal and cultural education, so-called, is to retain the time-honored position of humanistic and scientific knowledge in the curriculum, to withstand the onslaught of this new and somewhat sophomoric knowledge. The exponents of these older forms of knowledge seem to believe that there is something intrinsically fine, noble and dignified in old knowledge and something cheap and trivial in new knowledge. This is a long drawn-out, and oft-repeated controversy in which we are not primarily interested here.

Very often industrial education is confused with vocational education, or rather perhaps, vocational education is confused with industrial education. They are not the same thing at all. Vocational education is hardly more concerned with industrial knowledge than with liberal and cultural subject matter. Vocational education is concerned with training the child for some specific vocation. It emphasizes the result as well as the process. If the vocation is that of a lawyer, doctor, preacher, engineer, or teacher the emphasis in the process will be largely upon humanistic and scientific knowledge, though industrial knowledge should by no means be neglected. If, on the other hand, the vocation is that of a barber, salesman, plumber, mechanic, or carpenter the emphasis will be upon what is commonly called industrial knowledge, though again, liberal knowledge and scientific knowledge are both necessary and desirable.

Now, vocational education is not a new movement or a new kind of education. The importance of training for the higher vocations has been definitely recognized by education in schools for law, medicine and theology that have been in existence for centuries. Normal schools are merely vocational schools. The first educational foundations in the new world were established to train lawyers, teachers and preachers for the colonies. Military and naval schools have long prepared the youth for the vocations of soldier and sailor. Writers and editors have received vocational training in so-called cultural colleges. Gradually schooling has been extended to prepare for the vocation of the engineer, the farmer, the business man and the mechanic. The purpose of vocational education as a present day movement is not to build up something new, but rather to extend and enlarge the range of vocations for which the old system prepares. There are thousands of other vocations today which need carefully prepared and thoroughly trained workers. And, as the educational system in the past has gradually included within its range the preparation of workers for higher pursuits, so also today the system is being extended to include preparation for these newer vocations that have arisen in connection with a factory system of production.

We may consider the present day tendency toward vocational education under two headings. First, it is proposed that the curricula of existing schools shall be further vocationalized; second, it is proposed that new educational institutions with vocational curricula shall be generally established at public expense.

The vocationalizing of the curricula of existing schools, it is argued, will induce more children to stay longer in school, and also equip such children with an "industrial intelligence" that will be of great aid to them in bridging the gap that now exists between the school and the work-shop. To this end many industrial courses have been, and are being worked out and tested. The introduction of commercial spelling, English, arithmetic, law and geography on the one hand, and of manual and domestic arts on the other, indicate the trend of the movement, which has for its purpose the modification of the present school curriculum along vocational lines.

In addition to modifying the present system, as indicated in the preceding paragraph, new types of schools have come into existence, institutions with curricula of a mechanical, commercial, agricultural, domestic and trade character, known as polytechnical schools with a variety of new courses providing a wide range of studies in order to prepare for a larger number of vocations.

—7—

Of late, however, we are beginning to realize that these two proposed solutions do not answer the whole question of vocational education. We are learning that the industrializing of existing curricula and the establishment of new schools with more strictly vocational courses of study are slow and expensive processes; that vocations change more rapidly than the schools are able to respond, and that continuation schools, even when generally established and with attendance made compulsory, do not succeed in reaching all boys and girls and giving them counsel and supervision during the earlier years of their wage-earning careers. It is conceded that the introduction of vocational education by setting up vocational schools has done, and will continue to do, much toward making education of practical value to many children. But, it is asked, Will it reach them all? Can you train for all the occupations they may enter? Certainly to do so would mean a tremendous system of schools when you consider there are not less than 2000 gainful occupations pursued by adults which require some degree of skill that must be learned in some way. In other words, it is doubtful if institutional schooling alone, even on a broad co-operative basis, will ever become a full substitute for apprenticeship. But vocational education aims at becoming a system of apprenticeship adequate to the changed industrial conditions of the twentieth century. It realizes that a new apprenticeship is imperative. It would, therefore, supplement the providing of vocational training by giving to all juveniles expert vocational guidance and systematic vocational placement. As described by Reginald Bray, "an apprenticeship system to be worthy of the name must satisfy three conditions. First, it must provide for the adequate supervision of boys and girls until they reach at least the age of eighteen. Such supervision must have respect both to their conduct and to their physical development.

Secondly, an apprenticeship system must offer full opportunities for training, both general and special—the training of a citizen and the training of the worker. And, lastly, it must lead forward to some opening in the ranks of adult labor, for which definite preparation has been made, and in which good character may find reasonable prospects of permanent employment. Supervision, training, the provision of a suitable opening—these must be regarded as the three essentials of a modern apprenticeship system." [1]

The question before us is, How can such an apprenticeship system be instituted? Vocational education attempts to solve the problem. We have already briefly described two methods that are beginning to be commonly used. Schools both general and special in character offer the desired training. Such schools to the extent of their existence may in addition to giving children vocational training, also supervise and place them in suitable openings. But such schools exist in but few places, for comparatively few children and even fewer vocations. Consequently, they offer but a partial solution to the whole question of apprenticeship and vocational education.

It is apparent then, that special agencies are needed to supervise children until they are at least 18 years of age, and to place them in suitable employments. Such agencies would aid in preserving, utilizing, and increasing the education children have already received upon leaving school by watching over and placing them in occupations for which they are, as far as it is possible to determine, both by nature and by acquired abilities, best adapted.

The general establishment of such agencies is then the third way by which the larger problem of vocational education may be solved. Such agencies are primarily informational and supervisory in character. They maintain no

---

[1] (Bray, Reginald A. Boy Labor and Apprenticeship, p. 2. Constable & Co., London, 1911.)

schools for the training of children and no shops and factories for their immediate or future employment. They aim, on the other hand, through the giving of expert and scientific counsel and information to make all children conscious of the vocational abilities and opportunities they individually possess; to direct them into suitable places for their progressive vocational training either in schools or in factories and work-shops, and, finally, to supervise them until they attain a sufficient degree of skill to insure permanent success.

The establishment of these agencies is just as important and necessary as a system of Industrial Trade Schools. Indeed, it may be argued, they are more important as they offer immediate and practical aid within the reach of all. The chief function of such agencies must be educational, and, therefore, they are properly considered as instruments directly furthering vocational education. In general these agencies are becoming known as Vocation Bureaus, or Juvenile Information and Employment Bureaus;—agencies for the vocational guidance of youth.

The giving of organized vocational guidance through such agencies is a very recent development. We first hear of it in France and Germany in connection with the work of the trade organizations, municipal labor exchanges and the authorities in charge of industrial education. In England, Scotland, and Wales it was extensively advocated from 1904 to 1908 and Parliament has since passed acts permitting both school and trade authorities to spend public funds for the maintenance of those bureaus. The movement began in America in Boston and New York City about 1908 and has since spread throughout the country. The local newspapers of more than forty towns and cities located in some sixteen states discussed various aspects of vocational guidance during the six months from Dec., 1911 to May, 1912. Chicago, Pittsburg, Cleveland, Philadelphia, Grand Rapids,

St. Louis, Jamestown, (N. Y.) and Waltham, (Mass.) are
conspicuous examples of cities in the United States that are
following the lead of Boston and New York. The movement to establish such Bureaus is so recent that most people
know nothing at all about it, and the few who have heard
of it are not quite clear as to its character. Indeed, it may
be questioned if many of its advocates realize its full social
significance. Time and space will not permit a description
in detail of the work of such agencies. The reader, who is
interested will do well to read Mr. Bloomfield's little book
entitled *The Vocational Guidance of Youth,* and to glance
through the 25th Annual Report of the United States Commissioner of Labor on *Industrial Education.* One section
of this volume is devoted to a discussion of vocational guidance in this country.

WHY CHILDREN LEAVE SCHOOL TO GO TO WORK

Enough has been said to show that the employment of
children is an educational as well as a labor problem. The
ranks of labor are filled by the on-coming generation of
children going out from the public schools. Nearly every
child sooner or later in life must work and earn in order to
live. The census of 1900 showed nearly thirty million
workers, ten years of age and over, engaged in gainful occupations. It is roughly estimated that these thirty million
workers were engaged in some thirteen thousand gainful
pursuits. About two thousand of these pursuits were high
grade or skilled, ten thousand were low grade or unskilled,
while approximately one thousand were unhealthy, immoral, or unusually dangerous. There are a few persons
who do not seriously begin to work and earn until they are
twenty, twenty-five, or thirty years old, and until they have
completed a high school, a college and a university course.
On the other hand, the vast majority of boys and girls begin

to earn money before they have completed the eight grades
of an elementary school.

It is very difficult to determine exactly the reasons why
a child leaves school to go to work. Some argue that children quit school because they have to work and earn, while
others argue that they are tired of, and dissatisfied with
the kind of schooling that is offered them. The following
very carefully constructed table covers the most important
reasons that appear practically everywhere. This table was
made after a very intensive study of 620 children in seven
different localities, taken from two northern and two southern states.

According to this table there are about twenty-five different reasons given by children for leaving school. These
twenty-five reasons are, however, reducible to about four
fundamental causes. Either their earnings are necessary, or
their help is desired, or they are dissatisfied with school, or
they prefer work. In general, we may conclude from a
study of this table that the child's own dissatisfaction with
school accounts for about one-third of the cases, and that
the other leading cause is a financial one, which accounts
for over one-half of the eliminations. When we go behind
these figures we find that the chief reason for dropping out
of school can be traced directly to a lack of parental control
and interest. The parents seem to be in an indifferent
frame of mind about their children's schooling after they
have reached the legal age. They seem to think that the
child should be allowed to do about as he desires, and that
it is injurious to force him to go to school against his will.
No general theory fits every case, and probably few children
leave school for any one reason. The child's reason for
leaving is usually a complex of causes no one of which by
itself would be sufficient. And the percentage who leave
for any given reason or group of reasons will, of course,

TABLE 1.—SUMMARY OF CAUSES FOR CHILDREN LEAVING SCHOOL[1]

Causes for children leaving school to go to work	Number	Per Cent
NECESSITY		
Earnings necessary to family support.,...	169	
Help needed at home	6	
Self support necessary	11	
Total	186	30.0
CHILD'S HELP DESIRED, THOUGH NOT NECESSARY		
In family support.........................	140	
To buy property...........................	12	
In house work............................	14	
To earn money for education of self, relative	7	
Total..............................	173	27.9
CHILD'S DISSATISFACTION WITH SCHOOL		
Tired of school..............................	35	
Disliked school (general manner of life there)	54	
Disliked teachers..........	31	
Disliked study.............................	16	
Could not learn	10	
Not promoted	5	
Too big for class.....................	14	
Total...................................	165	26.6
CHILD'S PREFERENCE FOR WORK		
Work preferred to school..................	44	
Spending money wanted.............	8	
Association desired with friends who work	9	
Total	61	9.8
OTHER CAUSES		
Ill health..................................	16	
To be kept off the street...	1	
To learn a trade or business...............	6	
To avoid vaccination.......................	2	
Removal of residence........	1	
Mother's disapproval of coeducation	1	
"Too much play"	1	
Company pressure......	7	
Total.................................	35	5.7
Grand Total........................	620	100.

[1] Women and Child Wage Earners in the United States, Vol. 7.
Conditions Under Which Children Leave School to go to Work.
Senate Document, No. 645, Government Printing Office, Washington, 1910.

vary somewhat with the economic status of the community in which the children live. In large cities such as Chicago, and St. Louis, and no doubt, in many of the sixteen or eighteen chief industrial centers of the State of Illinois, the percentage leaving from necessity will be larger than in smaller communities where the struggle for existence is less acute. The important point to be noted, however, is that there are cases of this kind in every community, which require the very careful attention of teachers, principals and superintendents of schools if the future well-being of the child is not ruthlessly sacrificed to the immediate need of the family.

The report cited above points with emphasis to the fact that there are not a few families in which there is a feeling that the child should be put to work at the earliest moment and his earnings turned into the family income. But the most apparent feature "was an indifference to education on the part of the parents and children alike, and a disposition on the part of the former to cut short the child's school days for entirely insufficient causes".

The Number of Children who Leave School

Regardless of the cause it is now a well established fact that a great number of children leave school before they have had an opportunity to master even the elementary tools of learning, and while they are yet very young. Mr. Thorndike[2] finds that very few children stop school before they are twelve years old, but that of 100 in school at nine years of age, 9 will leave when they are twelve years old, 18 when they are thirteen, 23 when they are fourteen, 17 when they are fifteen, 14 when they are sixteen, and 8 when they are seventeen. Most drop out when they are from thirteen to fifteen years of age, feeling that further school

---

[2]Thorndike, Edward Lee, The Elimination of Pupils from School, Government Printing Office, Washington, 1908.

attendance is not vital to their success, G. Stanley Hall[3] points out that there are over eighteen million school children in the United States, and that of this number seventeen million drop out of school as soon as or before the law permits. D. E. Hawkins[3] estimates that in the public schools of this country each pupil attends on the average $5\frac{1}{3}$ years of 200 days each, while the average compulsory attendance found for all states having compulsory laws is 7.2 years of 8 to 40 weeks each. The educational department of the International Committee of the Young Men's Christian Association[3] concludes that only about 5 per cent of the thirteen million young men of the country from twenty-one to thirty-five years of age have received in school any preparation for their occupations, and that only about 8 per cent of those who graduate from the elementary school enter the higher professions and business pursuits while most of the remaining 92 per cent take up some industrial occupation.

According to these figures our public schools give great attention to the two million children who enter professional callings, and scarely any worthy the name to the twenty-eight million who engage in industrial occupations. It is thought that at least four million young people in this country leave elementary schools each year to enter the industries with no preparation for their work. In the United States over $30 is spent annually on the education of each child in regular school attendance. The average child receives about six years of instruction which cost $180. Each year these four million children representing the enormous expenditure of $720,000,000., are eliminated from the authority, discipline, and training of the schools and are thrown practically upon their own resources and responsibility. Annually this army of children pour out of schools to remain idle, or to enlist in almost every form of

3Hall, G. Stanley, Educational Problems, Vol. 1, pp. 544-6.

industrial activity. They run errands, carry messages, deliver parcels, address and copy letters, dig coal, work on farms, in shops and in the factories, and in hundreds of other ways enter upon their wage-earning careers. These four million children represent the most helpless and unfriended portion of the new recruits for the labor market. No systematic and positive effort is made, except here and there in a very few large cities, to guide or direct these school-leaving children into stimulating and educative employments and away from enervating and uneducative forms of labor. The deplorable fact is apparent "that the state largely abandons all interest in the child who leaves school after he is fourteen years old, and leaves him to waste the very expensive education it has given him as the most casual circumstances shall direct."[4] When the cost of their education is taken into account, "they represent an appalling waste of resources which no nation can or ought to afford."[4] The State moulds the training and education of children until they are fourteen, but permits chance circumstances to make or mar their careers thereafter.

Each year thousands of these well-equipped intelligent children are thrown on the labor market to engage in a blind, chaotic struggle for employment; and, as they depend for guidance either on the limited knowledge of their parents, or upon their own capricious inclinations, "it is not surprising that they so often fall easy prey to greedy exploiters, or to their efforts to earn wages in poor pursuits in support of their own immediate necessities."[4] The ignorance of parents, and sometimes their need and greed; the unscrupulousness of many employers, and the natural regardlessness of the children themselves succeed each year in wrecking promising lives by the thousands. In this struggle the State has offered these children neither guidance nor train-

---

[4] Knowles, Junior Labor Exchanges. p. 9.

ing, though it has vaguely and negatively recognized the problem and its duty respecting it in child labor legislation; yet, after undertaking the enormous trouble and expense of their education it has been content, until very recently at least, to stand by and see much of its effort wasted for the want of continuous vocational guidance, vocational training and after-care. The period of life when education is most needed, education is most lacking. "This most educable period of life is now most neglected."[3]

The right and duty of the State to safeguard its young citizens is commonly acknowledged. The right of youths to engage in gainful occupations has been in the past, and is now, fully recognized. Children are the wards of the State, and the State is in duty bound to exercise the parental authority vested in it. There is an old axiom that says: "If a community neglects its citizens when they are young, that community cannot complain if it is neglected by those children when they are older." The community must insure these children, both for individual and for social safety and progress, proper physical and mental development, and also suitable and promising employment.

Now, a proper amount and a proper kind of work under proper conditions is an undoubted good to be striven for in the education of youth. As Mr. Lindslay has written: "In the social economy of primitive peoples children began to share the labor of the family or of the clan at a very early age. It is instinctive on the part of even very immature boys and girls to participate in the activities about them, to imitate occupational pursuits, to yield to authority and direction, and through these associations and activities to obtain a certain degree of education on a natural scale. It is also customary, if not instinctive, for their elders to assign them tasks, and to encourage their occupational efforts, and to contribute in other ways to their education.

There is no evidence that such industrial participation has often been harmful. In fact, it is quite generally recognized that the sharing of economic activities is quite essential to the complete development of children from even five and six years of age onward. The labor of children under humane conditions has been traditionally established, and has not been in general an evil."[5]

Again, the individual discipline offered by suitable work is indispensable in every respect. The child must become self-sustaining, and the association through labor with men and women who are self-reliant and self-respecting members of society is of great educational value. The child needs a certain amount of work, both for his physical and mental well-being, and also in order that he may learn in advance how to earn a living. But unreasonable amounts of work, and unwholesome kinds of work, under bad conditions are evils to be socially combatted. The energy and youth of children should not be wasted in highly monotonous and uneducative employments. Thousands of children born in the United States, and children who have come here in early childhood, are unable to get along well in school, drop out and enter the lowest forms of unskilled work. You cannot keep some children in school any more than you can keep some children out of school. Many children have no real intellectual interests. Very few have tastes or abilities for learning in itself. Most children are in school to get something out of it and not merely for its own sake. "The drill to which they are subjected, and the foreign nature of the studies which they are forced to pursue, become irksome with the growth of adolescent conciousness." With the limited instruction which he is able to acquire in six years the average boy goes out into the world to engage in the business of making a living.

[5] Cyclopedia of Education, Child Labor

He is at best but poorly equipped with the fundamental intellectual tools. He possesses little or no knowledge at all of the vast, complex, intricate industrial and commercial life which has grown up in America during the last century. These children at the ages of twelve, thirteen, fourteen, fifteen, and older, retarded in their school work, are finally eliminated, and forced to remain idle or get a job and earn their own living.

At present when they leave school we say good-bye to them, and often, I fear, breathe a sigh of relief. We are not always sorry to see them go. We make no attempt to follow them up. We do not know, in most cases, what becomes of them industrially. We hope, with that serene faith so necessary in so many problems of life, that the world will not deal too harshly with them, and that they will ultimately become good and successful citizens.

We have studied elimination and retardation, and now we are beginning to study the causes of elimination, but as yet, we have not seriously studied the vocations as possible educational agencies. Yet, it is almost trite to say that a person's vocation is the greatest means of education that exists in his life if that vocation is carefully chosen and perfectly appreciated. We think of the home, and of the church, and the school as educational agencies. Why not also think of the job, the occupation, the vocation, the career as possibly on a par with, or superior to, these recognized agencies when fully appreciated and used for educational ends? At present we neglect it. We do not take a post-graduate interest in our public school children. We let them go and trust to providence or fate, and in the end marvel that society possesses so many unemployed and unfit workers. Society, and the schools as a social institution and instrument, until quite recently have not been, and indeed, generally speaking are not yet conscious of the waste produced by this failure to use the job and the career as a means of educating children.

This is one of the largest problems before the educator today. We have become a great factory nation. Industries are no longer simple but very complex. Machinery has replaced handicraft, and institutional training is beginning to replace apprenticeship. The child that goes to work today at the age of fourteen must almost invariably go into unskilled occupations. Such unskilled occupations offer little training of value, and for the most part, no opportunity for much advancement. The child while in school gives only 6 to 8 hours, five days a week to his or her school work, but on leaving and beginning to work, he or she is forced to spend 8 to 10 hours, and often as many as 12 hours daily, six days in the week, on the job. The child spends more time in work than in any other single activity and nearly as much as in all other forms of activity combined. The character of the occupation that a boy or a girl enters upon leaving school is, therefore, of the greatest importance. It should be a moral rather than an immoral pursuit; it should be a high grade rather than a low grade line of work; it should be promising rather than an unpromising employment; it should be a skilled rather than an unskilled job; a suitable rather than an unsuitable position; in a word, it should be a highly educative rather than a highly uneducative occupation.

If the reader is not already convinced that vocational guidance is needed in connection with public school systems in order to bridge the gap that now exists between life in the schoolroom and life in the vocations, an examination of the following data collected in St. Louis may serve as additional information and argument upon this question.

The First Occupation of School-Leaving Children

The following study shows very clearly what occupations city children, fourteen to sixteen years of age, enter upon leaving school. The city of St. Louis was chosen because the facts were easily obtainable. No systematic effort was made to guide or direct these children into or away from these occupations. Therefore, the list fairly represents the child's choice or chance in a city where the vocational guidance of school children is not yet attempted.

First, is shown the actual occupations boys and girls go into on leaving school after complying with the Compulsory Attendance and Child Labor Laws. Then a study of the popular occupations is made, demonstrating to what degree the school grade attained by the child indicates a superior occupation for that child under the present archaic methods of marketing his or her labor. The data used was secured by the writer in person from the office of the Compulsory Attendance Department of St. Louis.

In the city of St. Louis no child under the age of fourteen can be legally employed, permitted or suffered to work in any gainful occupation, except in agricultural pursuits, and in domestic service.

Children between fourteen and sixteen years of age must secure an employment certificate and work regularly in order to be released from school attendance. Employment certificates are issued by the attendance officer under the Superintendent of Public Instruction.

The issuing officer must certify, among other requirements, that the child has personally appeared before him, and has been examined and found able to read and write legibly simple sentences in the English language. He must further certify that in his opinion the child is fourteen years of age or over, has reached the normal development of a child of that age, is in sufficiently sound health and physically able to perform the work which he or she intends to do, which, according to the statement of the child is—(here is inserted the kind of work the child intends to perform). The law governing the issuance of employment certificates to minors in most states does not require the child to state the kind of work he is entering. This is a wiser law. It believes it is necessary to know what a child is going to do in order to be able to know whether that child is sufficiently healthy and physically able to perform the work he is leaving school to take.

A certificate of employment is not granted to a child unless that child has complied with this last requirement. It is not the duty of anybody to follow up these children in order to determine whether or not they get or take the kind of work they say they are going to take. It is probable that some of them do not. The officers in charge, who from their larger experience, would naturally be the most suspicious of the statements of the parents and the children are quite sure that not more than one in fifty of these children misrepresent the truth. The field work that these officers perform during the day and night looking after delinquency and truancy gives them an accurate basis for their judgment. It seems reasonable to assume that in nine cases out of ten the child takes the position stated. In many cases, as will be seen later on, the child has no definite agreement with the employer and no knowledge of the particular kind of work he or she will be required to do in that employment. He has only the vague promise of employment provided he can secure a certificate.

The usual method of securing a certificate may be briefly described as follows: The child, either from choice, necessity, or other causes, feels he must go to work. He is fourteen years old. Most of his companions are going to work, or are already at work, as we have already seen. No one knows very accurately why children leave school. The probabilities are that a large percent of those leaving are dissatisfied with school and feel that they must get into something more worth while. Work is their only escape, as idleness is illegal between the ages of fourteen and sixteen. These children leave every grade of the public school as will be seen later in this discussion. They talk to their teacher about their intentions, and he in turn, may interview the visiting parent. The teacher may encourage or discourage the child in his endeavor to leave school. Usually, however, the child is discouraged. If he persists he is sent to the principal or clerk of the school and a certificate of his age and attendance is given him. Armed with this document he looks up a job (provided he has not already secured one) and then applies for an employment certificate. If this certificate is granted him, as it is in nine cases out of ten, he goes to work without further hindrance.

It is the business of no one to accurately inform such children concerning the occupations open to them. No literature is handed them concerning desirable vocations: no advice is offered them regarding unskilled and skilled or highly skilled employments. They are not told about the "blind alley" jobs. No one looks after them systematically, following them from the door of the Employment Certificate Office into the jobs which necessity or choice cause them to accept. They have not read about the industrial and commercial life of the city in which they live. The school has not made it a *part of its business* to give guidance, provide training and secure positions for these children. They find their own jobs and take the jobs they can find quickly. They are, therefore, fair examples of what happens in the absence of vocational guidance and training

GRADES LEFT—From June 1, 1911 to March 1, 1912, 4386 children left the various schools of St. Louis, took employment certificates and went to work. Of this number 2703 or about 62% were boys, and 1683 or a little more than 38% were girls. Some idea of the number leaving each of the grades 'may be gained by a glance at the following table of distribution by grade and sex.

TABLE 2.—GRADE OF BOYS AND GIRLS RECEIVING EMPLOYMENT
CERTIFICATES, ST. LOUIS.
1911–1912

Grade	Boys, No. of,	Girls, No. of,	Total	Per cent
1	6	7	13	.29
2	14	14	28	.64
3	85	47	132	3.02
4	293	153	446	9.79
5	511	332	843	19.29
6	641	373	1014	23.21
7	582	398	980	22.43
8	463	325	788	18.04
9	72	22	94	2.15
10	15	22	17	.38
11	7	0	7	.16
Unknown	14	10	24	
Total	2703	1683	4386	
Per Cent	62%	38%	100%	
Median	6.67 grade	6.72 grade	6.71 grade	

Almost fourteen per cent of these children had not reached the fifth grade, 38% had not reached the sixth grade, 56% had not reached the seventh grade, and 78% had not finished the seventh grade. Yet all of these children were from 14 to 16 years of age, and, according to average figures, should have been in the eighth grade. The 15% who had not reached the fifth grade were from four to seven years over age for their grades; the 33% who had not reached the sixth grade were from three to seven years over age, and the 78% who had not finished the seventh grade were from one to seven years over age for their grades. The average child of this group is approximately two years over age for the grade attained. The median child in this group leaves school after the 6.71 grade, or after getting a little over half through the sixth grade; the median boy the 6.67 grade, or about six and a half grades, while the median girl is scarcely better off, having reached only the 6.72 grade. These facts are in essential agreement with those reported by the Attendance Department in its annual report for 1911. According to that report, the median 14 to 16 years old child leaving school to go to work has attained the 6.43 grade. This means that 50% of these children had attained less than the 6.43 grade, and 50% more than the 6.43 grade.

Roughly speaking, these 14 to 16 year old children, who are leaving school to go to work, have received that amount of school instruction contained in 6½ to 6¾ grades of the elementary school. They have about a six and a half grade education and are from one and a half to two and a half years over age. The amount of education that a boy has acquired is about one-eighth of a grade less than which a girl received. In other words, there is practically no difference in the education of a boy and a girl belonging to this group. This is of interest in view of the fact that it is often argued that the girls of the employment certificate class are better equipped than the boys in respect to the amount of school work accomplished. This is not true if these figures are correct. The boys and girls of this group begin their vocational life with practically the same amount of education, are about the same age, and have made about equal progress through the grades.

OCCUPATIONS ENTERED.—A brief glance at the list of occupations that these unguided children go into upon leaving school is next in order. These 4368 children, whose school history we have briefly described, and in whose oc-

cupational history we are interested, immediately entered
nearly one hundred different pursuits

TABLE 3.—THE. NINETEEN MOST POPULAR OCCUPATIONS

Occupation	No. Boys	No. Girls	Total
Helpers	1136	739	1875
Errand boys and girls..............	424	12	436
Messengers..........................	236		236
Office work..........................	321	64	385
Clerks, (Shipping, stock, sales, etc.)..	90	37	127
Cash boys and girls...............	14	261	275
Wrappers and packers (bundle)...	81	78	159
Wagon and delivery........... ..	122	1	123
Sewing	6	100	106
Factory workers, operators, shop work..........................	49	52	101
Apprentices	13	41	54
Labeling (pasting and cutting labels)	14	40	54
Box makers (paper boxes, nailing).	27	13	40
Millinery...........................	2	86	88
Laundry work (shakers, folders, manglers, sprinklers)	8	17	25
Confectioners (nut pickers), (candy)	3	40	43
Bottling (including bottle washing)	21	1	22
Bell and hall boys	12		12
Counting and sorting ....,.	4	10	14
Total.......................	2583	1592	4175

These nineteen occupations include 95% of the whole
group. The remaining are scattered through some sixty-
six lines of work. The occupations which they intended
to enter are as follows:

Nine waiters and waitresses; eight each, stenography
and folding circulars; seven each, cutting (thread, paper,
samples), and house work; six each, wire frame work, check-
ing, flower work, and printing; five each, selling papers,
tailoring, dyeing and cleaning, and stacking (wheels, boxes,
barrels); four each, floor boys, stamping, peddling, and
painting and varnishing; three each, tagging, trucking,

marking, making buttons, making baskets, dressmaking, bookbinding, carpentering, coopering, hostler, and janitorial; two each, sawyer, hat, cap, and bonnet maker, buyer, bootblack, usher, collector, horse-shoeing, nursing, hair work and sample room. The remaining thirty pursuits are each represented by one child, baker, making trunks, bag tyer, work in cooler, electrician, police department, brusher, surveyor, pail maker, stencil maker, brush maker, washboard maker, telegraph operator, soda fountain, nigger stand, guager, pad-maker, glass-worker, brass dryer, upholsterer, machinist, window dresser, iron worker, umbrella tipper, awning maker, feather work, telephone operator, inspector, making calenders, and sign carrier.

The boys go into a greater variety of occupations than the girls, as is shown by both of these lists. There are two among the first nineteen pursuits, that of messenger and bell boy, that girls do not enter. On the other hand six boys are doing factory sewing, and two boys do millinery work, occupations in which one might expect to find only girls. Of the remaining sixty-six pursuits, forty-three are represented only by boys and twelve by girls. Those in which boys alone are found are news-boys, trucking, stacking (wheels, boxes, barrels), carpentering, baker, sawyer, making trunks, hat maker, cooper, bag tyer, painters (varnishing), horse-shoeing, work in cooler, electrician, buyer, hostler, book-binding, floor boy, police department, bootblack, brusher, surveyor, pail maker, telegraph operator, soda fountain, nigger stand, guager, collector, pad maker, glass worker, brass dryer, upholsterer, window dresser, sign carrier, iron worker, and umbrella tipper.

Those in which girls alone are found are: house work, nursing, making awnings, making calenders, feather work, hairwork, flower work, dress-making, tailoring, telephone operator, and inspector.

From such figures it may be seen that the boys have almost two chances to the girls' one in respect to the number of different pursuits they may enter. The boys of this grade enter some seventy-three different occupations, while the girls enter but forty. Apparently the girls are more restricted than the boys in their choice of occupations. Undoubtedly both need to be directed away from many of the pursuits listed above.

It is very difficult to say which of these occupations are skilled and which are unskilled. No one seems to have a definition that is easily and accurately applied. The general definition of the unskilled vocation, according to the Report of the Commissioner on Industrial and Technical Education, 1906, (Mass.), is any one in which the work consists in a repetition of a single or a few simple operations easily and quickly learned, and in which one operation is not definitely co-ordinated with all those that precede and follow. The grade of ability and the responsibility required is low and the wages are correspondingly low. The distinction made by this report between a low-grade skilled industry and a high grade industry, is that the former does not require a first class workman to have a knowledge of all the operations, nor do the processes require a great amount of skill, and one is usually able to learn such operations in a few months at the most. A vocation of a high grade is one in which the skill must be acquired by some years of experience, or school training, or both.

According to the Massachusetts report, 33% of the children of the state who begin work between the ages of fourteen and sixteen are employed in unskilled industries, and sixty-five per cent in low grade skilled industries. The nature of our data precludes the possibility of a rigid classification on the basis of the degree of skill required. We are not always sure just where each case belongs. For instance, is the occupation of a waiter an unskilled or a low grade occupation? We have called it a low grade skilled occupation. Unfortunately the Massachusetts report does not give a key to its classification, and I have not been able to find one elsewhere. However, accepting the above definition, and, in a more or less arbitrary manner, classifying the occupations of these St. Louis children accordingly, we find that we have thirty-eight unskilled, thirty-six low grade skilled, and thirteen high grade skilled occupations, as will be seen in Table IV.

We have already seen that 95% of these children entered nineteen different employments. Of these 90% are in unskilled pursuits. The remaining 10% are in low-grade or high-grade skilled occupations; a little more than 3% in the latter.

TABLE IV.

NINETEEN MOST POPULAR OCCUPATIONS CLASSIFIED

Unskilled		Low-grade skilled		High-grade skilled	
Helpers.........	1875	Clerks (shipping, sales, stock)	127	Millinery.........	88
Errand boys and girls...........	436	Sewing (factory).	106	Apprentices..... ..	54
Office work......	385	Box makers.......	40		
Cash boys, girls..	275				
Messengers.......	236				
Wrappers	159				
Wagon boys.....	123				
Factory workers.	101				
Labelling........	54				
Bottling	26				
Confectioners...	43				
Laundry.........	25				
Counting, sorting	14				
Hall, bell boys...	12				
Total..	3764	....	273	....	142

TABLE V.

SIXTY-SIX REMAINING OCCUPATIONS CLASSIFIED.

Unskilled	Low-grade skilled	High-grade skilled
Folding circulars... 8	Wire frame workers 6	Stenography....... 8
Checking............ 6	Flower makers...... 6	Printer (typist)... 6
Cutting........., .. 7	Waiters and	Carpenter (cabinet
News boys (dealers) 5	waitresses......... 9	making.......... 3
Tagging............. 3	Baker 1	Surveyor.......... 1
Trucking............ 3	Trunk makers....... 1	Telegraph operator 1
Stacking.......... .. 6	Hat, cap, bonnet..... 2	Machinist 1
Marker.............. 3	Coopers 2	Dress-making..... 2
Bag tyer 1	Painter (carriage	Tailoring.......... 5
Work in cooler..... 1	varnish)......... 4	Sawyer............... 2
Hostler....... 3	Basket maker....... 3	Electrician......... 1
Floor boy........... 4	Horse-shoeing 2	Bookbinding....... 2
Police Dept......... 1	Buyer 2	
Boot-black.......... 1	Pail maker 1	
Brusher............. 1	Button maker 3	
Usher 2	Dyeing and cleaning 6	
Peddler............. 4	Stencil cutter........ 1	
Stamping........... 4	Brush maker.. 1	
Sample room........ 2	Wash-board maker. 1	
Soda fountain...... 1	Guager.............. 1	
Nigger stand....... 1	Collector 2	
House work........ 7	Pad maker.... 1	
Janitorial 3	Glass worker........ 1	
Sign carrier........ 1	Dyeing brass........ 1	
	Upholsterer......... 1	
	Window dresser.... 1	
	Iron worker........ 1	
	Umbrella tipper..... 1	
	Nurse....... 2	
	Feather worker..... 1	
	Hair work.......... 2	
Total............ 78	 66	 32

A still more startling fact is that nearly 70% of the children, who are leaving the St. Louis public schools and going to work, are entering occupations that demand merely fetching and carrying; such, for instance, as delivery boy, messengers, cash boy or girl, or errand boy or girl, wagon boy, hall boy, and bell boy. These are all unskilled occupations. The chief duties of the person pursuing them is to wait upon the casual needs of the employer. At least seven out of ten of these St. Louis children begin their vocational career in work of this kind. It may be well to ask if the' schools exist to train errand boys, messengers, cash boys and girls—in other words, unskilled labor. For what vocations then does the school exist?

GRADE LEFT IN RELATION TO OCCUPATION ENTERED—The next part of this study deals with the grades attained by the children pursuing the nineteen more popular occupations. Each of these occupations is represented by at least ten children. The grade that a child has attained is one of the facts required by the officer issuing the Employment Certificate. A certain percentage of the children have graduated from the grammar school, and a few are leaving the first, second, and third years of high school. For the purpose of this study, a child who has graduated from the grammar school is considered as having attained the ninth grade, or first year of high school. A child who is in the first year of high school is also in the ninth grade, a child in the second year of high school is in the tenth, etc. The following table shows the nineteen leading occupations that these children pursue, and the number leaving each of the grades and entering a given vocation.

Each of sixteen of these occupations are represented by forty or more workers. I have considered forty or more children in a given occupation a sufficient number to make my conclusions comparable. Clerks, office workers, milliners, apprentices, and labelers attain on the average 7.8 grades. Ranked by median grades attained, we have the series as follows: office work. 7.83; clerks, 7.77; apprentices, 7.66; milliners, 7.5; and labeler, 7.07. On the other hand, wrappers, factory workers, errand boys, messengers, wagon

TABLE VI.—RELATION OF OCCUPATION CHOSEN TO GRADE LEFT

Occupation	Total B and G	1	2	3	4	5	6	7	8	Gr.	9	10	11	Med.	Un.
Helpers	1875	10	18	80	216	404	480	382	127	124	20	3		6.42	9
Clerks	127		1	1	1	8	24	35	36	9	10	3		7.77	
Mfrs	159			6	16	33	29	36	22	13	4	1	1	6.79	2
Factory work	101		1	2	9	21	30	21	10	7	1			6.93	2
Errand boys and girls	436		1	13	40	94	125	109	54	27	9	1	1	6.55	
Office work	385		1	1	11	34	67	92	71	57	39	7	3	7.83	
Cash girls and boys	275			3	23	61	64	68	34	18	3			6.78	1
Messengers	236		1	1	33	48	64	48	15	16	4	1		6.50	3
Wagon	123			4	17	33	29	26	12	13				6.34	
Sewing	106	1	5	4	13	18	26	8	28	8		2		6.65	
Millinery	88		1	1	1	12	13	32	15	13	1	1		7.50	1
Apprentices	54		1	1	2	9	16	18	12	5			1	7.66	
Labeling	54		1	1	1	4	6	14	11	1	1		1	7.07	
Bottling	26	1	1	1	5	9	16	3						6.16	
Confectioner	43			1	10	4	6	10	1	2	1			5.75	
Box maker	40		2		10	12	7	6	6	1	1			6.16	
Sorting and ounting	14			2	5	10	6			1				7.16	
Bell and hall boys	12				3	2	3	2	3	2	1			7.00	
Laundry work	25			2	4	4	7	5	3	2	1			6.28	

boys, cash girls and boys, factory workers, and bottlers average between 6 and 6.93 grades. Confectioners average 5.75 grade. However, 37 of those listed as confectioners were nut pickers, which requires practically no skill.

SUMMARY—The significant facts about this study may be summarized briefly:

1. That, about 62% of the St. Louis children between 14 and 16 years of age receiving employment certificates are boys and 38% are girls. ·

2. That, 33% of these children had not reached the sixth grade, 56% had not reached the seventh grade, and 78% had not finished the seventh grade.

3. That, the median (average) child had received on leaving school that amount of education contained in from six and one-half to six and three-fourths grades of the elementary school.

4. That, there is practically no difference in the amount of education received by boys and girls of this group.

5. That, these unguided children immediately entered 85 different occupations; 95% in nineteen different pursuits and 5% in sixty-six additional lines.

6. That, the boys entered 73 out of the 85 occupations represented, while the girls entered but 40. The girls are, therefore, about twice as restricted as the boys in their choice of pursuits.

7. That, by rough classification, about 90% of these children entered unskilled occupations; about 7% low grade skilled and less than 3% high-grade skilled work.

8. That, over 70% of these children entered occupations that demand merely fetching and carrying—such as delivery, cash, messenger, errand, wagon, hall and bell boy and girls service.

9. That, those children who are most successful in attaining a higher grade, tend to be more successful in selecting preferred occupations.

10. That, fetching and carrying occupations tend to be filled from the sixth grade, while clerks, office workers, milliners, and apprentices tend to be drawn from the seventh grade.

This study demonstrates very clearly what happens to children who leave school and enter vocational careers without direction or counsel. What might have happened to them had guidance been provided, can only be inferred. But it is safe to venture that the percentage of those entering unskilled and low-grade skilled industries would have been greatly decreased, and also that the fetching and carrying occupations, which are in every respect "blind alleys," would have been avoided in a large degree. Someone with the time might study an equal number of children leaving the schools of a city where guidance is provided, and contrast the two groups. Such a contrast would measure the kind and value of the guidance given. It would then be possible to know, to some degree, at least, how much a state or city could afford to spend instituting such guidance. At present we have a feeling that guidance is valuable but we are unable to say to what degree.

Conclusion

One English writer on the subject of juvenile labor says, "Just as the first few years of childhood are the most critical years for the physical well-being of the individual, the first few years after leaving school are the most critical for the moral and mental well-being of our working population." The same author argues that the existence of a well organized bureau in a community would help systemize the efforts made on behalf of young workers by parents, teachers, clergymen and philanthropic organizations. Such bureaus in the cities and larger towns would have several functions to perform. Such, for instance, as giving information about vocational schools located in various parts of the state and country: they would be able to advise with children before they left school and for a few years after they had entered industries, supplying to such children accurate information with regard to the qualifications required in various occupations, the wages paid, the prospects in various employments and the opportunity for promotion or advancement in those employments. They would be very helpful in getting children into better grades of work thus avoiding the pitfalls of blind alley occupations, or occupations that have no future. The director of such a bureau would keep a record of the children leaving the different schools, and also a record of that child's scholastic attainment so that from his expert knowledge of the local industries he would be in a position to advise children concerning suitable work and future schooling.

In England an act known as the "Choice of Employment Act" passed Parliament November 28, 1910 which accorded local boards of education control over a system of vocational bureaus which proposed "to give the boys and girls under 17 years of age information, advice and assistance with regard to the choice of a suitable employment."

The establishment of such bureaus was first suggested by Mrs. Gordon in Glasgow, Scotland, in 1904. Mrs. Gordon suggested that local boards of education should establish bureaus for the purpose of guiding boys and girls into suitable occupations on leaving school, or keeping them in sight until they were of an age to begin work for which each seemed best adapted. Since that time these bureaus have been established in nearly two hundred cities and towns of England. The general purpose of these bureaus is, as has already been stated, to lead all boys and girls, before and after they leave school, toward employments that will be profitable and congenial to them in their later life.

In view of the interest that is developed throughout Europe and America in this subject it is almost safe to predict that the time is not long distant when every large public school system in America will have a Vocational Bureau in intimate connection with its regular scholastic work. Through these bureaus the teachers will be able to extend their wholesome influence far into the after-life of the children who come under their supervision.

THE NORMAL
SCHOOL BULLETIN

EASTERN ILLINOIS STATE NORMAL
SCHOOL, CHARLESTON

OCTOBER FIRST, 1914
NUMBER 46

MATERIAL ON GEOGRAPHY
which may be obtained free or at small cost

by

MARY JOSEPHINE BOOTH, A.B., B.L.S.
Librarian, Eastern Illinois State Normal School

THE NORMAL SCHOOL BULLETIN

PUBLISHED BY THE EASTERN ILLINOIS STATE NORMAL SCHOOL

Entered March 5, 1902, as second-class matter, at the post office at Charleston, Illinois.
Act of Congress, July 16, 1894.

CHARLESTON, ILLINOIS, OCTOBER 1, 1914   No. 46

MATERIAL ON GEOGRAPHY
which may be obtained free or at small cost

by

MARY JOSEPHINE BOOTH
A.B., Beloit College; B.L.S., University of Illinois,
Librarian, Eastern Illinois State Normal School

EASTERN ILLINOIS STATE NORMAL SCHOOL
CHARLESTON
1914

TABLE OF CONTENTS

PREFACE

Publications of this description are usually issued in the form of well illustrated pamphlets and will supplement with little expense the books on geography used in the class room. They come from several sources, the United States government, the different state governments, railroads, steamship lines, manufacturing firms, and chambers of commerce of cities and towns.

To find out where material of this sort may be obtained requires both time and effort. Each month consult the Monthly catalogue of United States public documents, and the Monthly list of state publications, both published by the Superintendent of Documents, Washington, D. C. Read the advertisements of railroads and of steamship companies appearing in magazines and newspapers, which often offer to send free or for postage descriptive booklets. These advertisements change with the seasons and in the course of a year will include almost all parts of the world. In the columns of *Public Libraries, The Library Journal, The Wisconsin Library Bulletin,* and other periodicals are often found items giving the names of recent pamphlets.

Write to your congressman for any desired pamphlets published by the United States government. If he has copies at his disposal, he will send them free, but if not, the Superintendent of Documents, Washington, will supply them for the price stated in this list. The publications of the Pan American Union may also be obtained free from your congressman. Address the proper department for the state publications, enclosing postage. Write to railroads and steamship lines giving the names of the pamphlets desired and enclose postage. If you want to obtain the most recent material write for a list of publications and choose the ones needed, for new booklets are being frequently issued. Because of the ephemeral nature of many of these publications certain titles given in this list may even now be out of print. Frequently new booklets will be issued to replace them and on this account it is usually better, when writing for a certain title, to add a request for "other similar publications." Some of the European railroads, trans-atlantic steamship lines, and tourist agencies will be unable to supply all the titles listed because of the war in Europe. Their addresses have been given with the expectation that they will be of use in the future. Those titles issued by these agencies, which are definitely known to be available, are so designated.

County and city superintendents of schools may be able to obtain several copies of the material in this list and keep it in a convenient place for the use of teachers under their direction.

The first edition of this list was published in the *Wisconsin Library Bulletin* for January-February, 1912. A revised list was published in the *Journal of Geography,* January, 1914, a number of the new titles having been suggested by Miss Adelaide R. Hasse, Chief, Public Documents Department, New York Public Library. It was reprinted by the American Library Association Publishing Board, 78 East Washington Street, Chicago. The new titles in this list are largely pamphlets issued by commercial clubs and chambers of commerce.

List of Abbreviations

The usual abbreviations of states and months are used.

agric.—agriculture

Amer.—American

ass'n—association

ave.—avenue

bldg—building

Bost.—Boston, Mass.

bull.—bulletin

bur.—bureau

c.—cent, copyright

Chic.—Chicago, Ill.

circ.—circular

cm.—centimeter

co.—company

cong.—congress

d.—penny, pence=2c.

dep't—department

div.—division

doc.—document

ed.—edition

educ.—education

Lond.—London, England

Minn.—Minneapolis, Minn.

n. d.—no date

no.—number

N. Y.—New York, N. Y.

Phil.—Philadelphia, Penn.

pt—part

R. R.—railroad, railway

rep't—report

S. S.—steamship

ser.—series

sess.—session

st.—street

Sup't of doc.—Superintendent of documents

s.—shilling=25c.

univ.—university

v.—volume

Wash.—Washington, D. C.

GENERAL LIST

Bibliography

Commercial and agricultural organizations of the United States. 1913. Miscellaneous ser. 8. Foreign and domestic commerce bur. Wash. Senate doc. 1109. 62nd cong. 3rd sess. or, Sup't of doc. Wash. 15c.

Commercial organizations in southern and western cities by G. W. Doonan. 1914. Special agents ser. 79. Foreign and domestic commerce bur. Wash. or, Sup't of doc. Wash. 10c.

These two lists of commercial organizations are useful in obtaining names and addresses of chambers of commerce and commercial clubs. They do not list publications.

Geography, in Frederick K. Noyes, Teaching material in government publications. pp. 32-44. 1913. Bull. 1913, no. 47. Bur. of educ. Wash. or, Sup't of doc. Wash. 10c.

Includes physical, political and commercial geography and maps.

Geography and explorations; list of United States government publications. 1911. Sup't of doc. Wash.

Maps published by the United States government. 1913. Sup't of doc. Wash.

Periodicals

Agwi steamship news, monthly. Agwi steamship news, 165 Broadway, N. Y.

The earth, monthly. The earth, 1118 Railway exchange, Chic. 25c. a year.

K. C. S. current events, an industrial and agricultural magazine, quarterly. Kansas City southern R. R. Kansas City, Mo.

North German Lloyd bulletin, monthly. North German Lloyd bulletin, 5 Broadway, N. Y. 24c. a year.

AFRICA, EAST

East Africa protectorate. 1908. Emigrants' information office,
34 Broadway, Westminster, S. W. Lond. 6d.

Africa, South, see South Africa.

AFRICA, WEST

Colonial west Africa (with map). 1912. Elder Dempster and co.
lld, Colonial house, Liverpool, England, or, 6 St Sacrament
st. Montreal, Can. 1s. Also other publications.

Handbook of information for passengers of the Deutsche Ost-
Afrika-linie. 1914. Tourist office, Hamburg-Amer. line,
N. Y. or, Ellis, Kislingbury and co. 4 St Mary Axe E. C. Lond.

Notes on the West African colonies. 1911. Emigrants' information office, 34 Broadway, Westminster, S. W. Lond. 6d.

ALABAMA

Alabama. 1911. State dep't of immigration, Montgomery. Also
other publications.

Jefferson county and Birmingham, Alabama. 1911. Chamber of
commerce, Birmingham. Also other publications.

Mobile, Alabama. n. d. Chamber of commerce and business
league, Mobile. Also other publications.

ALASKA

Alaska fisheries and fur industries in 1913. (annual) 1914.
Doc. 797. Bur. of fisheries, Wash.

Alaska, glaciers and ice fields. (latest ed.) Alaska S. S. co.
Seattle, Wash. Also other publications.

Alaska mining industry in 1911 and railway routes in Alaska by
A. H. Brooks. 1912. Bull. 520 A. Geological survey, Wash.
or Sup't of doc. Wash. 20c.

Alaska, our frontier wonderland. 1914. Alaska bur. Seattle
chamber of commerce, Seattle, Wash. 10c.

Coastal glaciers of Prince William sound and Kenai peninsula
by U. S. Grant and D. F. Higgins. 1913. Bull. 526. Geological survey, Wash. or, Sup't of doc. Wash. 30c.

Commerce and industries of Alaska, Hawaii, Porto Rico, and the
Philippine islands. 1913. Special agents ser. 67. Bur. of
foreign and domestic commerce, Wash. or, Sup't of doc.
Wash. 10c.

Data relating to Alaska, resources, and progress. 1912. Senate
doc. 882. 62nd cong. 2nd sess. or, Sup't of doc. Wash. 5c.

General information regarding Alaska. 1914. Interior dep't, Wash.

Possible agricultural development in Alaska by Levi Chubbuck. 1914. Bull. 50. Div. of publications, Dep't of agric. Wash. or, Sup't of doc. Wash. 10c.

Bibliography

Alaska territory, list of public documents for sale by Sup't of doc. 1914. Sup't of doc. Wash.

ALBERTA

Official handbook of Alberta. (latest ed.) Dep't of agric. Edmonton. Also other publications.

ARGENTINE REPUBLIC

Argentine international trade. 1913. Distributed by Pan Amer. union, Wash.

Argentine Republic. 1908. Emigrants' information office, 34 Broadway, Westminster, S. W. Lond. 2d.

Argentine Republic; general descriptive data. 1913. Pan Amer. union, Wash.

The Argentine Republic in 1912. 1912. Distributed by Pan Amer. union, Wash.

Commerce of Argentine Republic. (annual) Pan Amer. union, Wash.

General description of Argentine Republic. 1913. Distributed by Pan Amer. union, Wash.

Trade development in Argentina by J. D. Whelpley. 1911. House doc. 1032, 61st cong. 3rd sess. Wash. Also Special agents ser. 43. Manufactures bur. Wash. or, Sup't of doc. Wash. 10c.

ARIZONA

Arizona, the newest state. n. d. Santa Fe, 1119 Railway exchange, Chic. Also other publications.

Glendale, Arizona. n. d. Board of trade, Glendale.

The new Arizona. (latest ed.) Southern Pacific R. R., Chic.

Phoenix, Arizona, city of progress. 1913. Board of trade, Phoenix. Also other publications.

Arizona, see also Casa Grande, Grand canyon of the Colorado.

ARKANSAS

Arkansas homes and harvests. n. d. Cotton belt route, St Louis, Mo. Also other publications.

Arkansas, the home of double crops. 1911. Rock Island lines, Chic. Also other publications.

Biennial rep't. (latest ed.) Bur. of mines and manufactures and agric. Little Rock.

General information regarding the Hot Springs of Arkansas. 1912. Dep't of the interior, Wash. or, Sup't of doc. Wash. 5c.

Missouri and Arkansas Ozarks. n. d. Frisco lines, St Louis, Mo.

The Ozark mountain region. (latest ed.) Kansas City southern R. R. Kansas City, Mo.

Southeastern Arkansas. n. d. Missouri Pacific-Iron Mountain R. R. St Louis, Mo. Also other publications describing different sections of the state.

AUSTRALIA

Australia, its resources, industries, and trade. 1911. Special consular rep'ts 47. Bur. of foreign and domestic commerce, Wash. or, Sup't of doc. Wash. 10c.

The Australian commonwealth; its resources and production. 1912. Commonwealth bur. of census and statistics, Melbourne.

AUSTRIA

Austria. n. d. Canadian Pacific R. R. Montreal, Can.

The South railway in Austria-Hungary, n. d., published by the South R. R. Vienna. Address Thos. Cook and son, 245 Broadway, N. Y. Also other publications.

Sport, fishing in Alpine Austria. n. d. edited by the I. and R. board of agric. Vienna. Address Thos. Cook and son, 245 Broadway, N. Y.

Traveling routes in Austria. n. d. issued by the I. R. Austrian state R. R. Vienna. Address Thos. Cook and son, 245 Broadway, N. Y.

BELGIUM

Belgium. n. d. Red star line, 9 Broadway, N. Y. Available.

Holidays abroad. 1912. Great eastern R. R. 261 Broadway, N. Y.

BOLIVIA

Bolivia; general descriptive data. 1913. Pan Amer. union, Wash.

Commerce of Bolivia. (annual) Pan Amer. union, Wash.

BRAZIL

Brazil; general descriptive data. 1913. Pan Amer. union, Wash.

Brazil in 1912. (annual) by J. C. Oakenfull. Distributed by Pan Amer. union, Wash.

Commerce of Brazil. (annual) Pan Amer. union, Wash.

Economic protection of the India rubber. 1912. Distributed by Pan Amer. union, Wash.

BRITISH COLUMBIA

Banff, Field, Glacier, etc. 2-10c. Soo line, Chic. Also other publications.

Canada's western heritage, British Columbia. 1912. Dep't of the interior, Ottawa, Can.

Handbook of British Columbia. 1913. Bur. of provincial information, Victoria. Also other publications.

Prince Rupert, British Columbia. 1911. Grand trunk Pacific R. R. Montreal, Can.

CALIFORNIA

California. 1910. Rock Island lines, Chic.

California for the tourist. 1910. Southern Pacific R. R. Chic. Also other publications.

The California lemon industry by G. H. Powell and F. O. Wallschlaeger. Bull. 9. Citrus protective league of California, Los Angeles.

California, resources and possibilities. (annual) California development board, San Francisco.

California south of Tehachapi. (latest ed.) Southern Pacific R. R. Chic.

The climate and weather of San Diego, California. 1913. Chamber of commerce, San Diego.

Climate of San Francisco by A. G. McAdie. 1913. Bull. 44. Weather bur. Wash. or, Sup't of doc. Wash. 5c.

Harbor development of San Francisco. 1913. Berkeley civic bull. v. 2, no. 5. 15 Dec. '13· City club of Berkeley, 1923 Dwight Way, Berkeley.

Los Angeles, city and county. 1913. Chamber of commerce, Los Angeles. Also other publications.

Oakland. (latest ed.) Chamber of commerce, Oakland.

Pasadena. n. d. Special no. of The Arrowhead, monthly published by Industrial dep't, San Pedro, Los Angeles and Salt Lake R. R. Los Angeles.

Pasadena, California. n. d. Board of trade, Pasadena.

Rep't. (latest ed.) State agric. society, Sacramento.

Rep't on Richmond harbor project by Haviland and Tibbetts. 1912. Haviland and Tibbetts, Alaska commercial bldg, San Francisco. Also other publications.

Sacramento valley. (latest ed.) Southern Pacific R. R. Chic.

Sacramento valley, California, n. d. Sunset magazine home-seekers' bur. San Francisco. Not the same as the preceding entry.

San Diego, California. n. d. Board of supervisors of San Diego county, or, Chamber of commerce of San Diego county, San Diego.

San Francisco. 1913. Chamber of commerce, San Francisco. Also other publications.

San Joaquin valley of California. n. d. Santa Fe, 1119 Railway exchange, Chic. Also other publications.

San José, Santa Clara county. n. d. Chamber of commerce, San José.

California, see also General Grant national park, Sequoia national park, Yosemite national park.

CANADA

Annual rep't. (latest ed.) Dep't of the interior, Ottawa. Also other publications.

Canada. (annual) Emigrants' information office. 34 Broadway, Westminster, S. W. Lond. 1d.

Commerce and industries of Canada and Newfoundland by A. Robinson. 1913. Special agents ser. 76. Foreign and domestic commerce bur. Wash. or, Sup't of doc. Wash. 10c.

Fur-farming in Canada by J. W. Jones. 1913. Commission of servation, Ottawa. 50c.

Geography of the Dominion of Canada. n. d. Dep't of the interior. Ottawa.

Guide books. 1913. Geological survey, Ottawa.

No. 1. Eastern Quebec and the maritime provinces. 2 pts.

No. 2. Eastern townships of Quebec and the eastern part of Ontario.

No. 3. Neighborhood of Montreal and Ottawa.

No. 4. Southwestern Ontario.

No. 5. Western peninsula of Ontario and Manitoulin island.

No. 6. Vicinity of Toronto, Muskota and Madoc.

No. 7. Sudbury, Cobalt and Porcupine.

No. 8. Toronto to Victoria and return via Canadian Pacific and Canadian Northern railways. 3 pts.

No. 9. Toronto to Victoria and return via Canadian Pacific, Grand Trunk Pacific and National trans-continental railways.

No. 10. Northern British Columbia and Yukon territory and along the north Pacific coast.

The material is largely geological but some parts are of general interest.

Land, a living, and wealth. n. d. Grand trunk Pacific R. R. Winnipeg, Manitoba.

Sea fisheries of eastern Canada. 1912. Commission of conservation. Ottawa.

CASA GRANDE

General information regarding the Casa Grande ruin, Arizona. 1913. Interior dep't, Wash. or, Sup't of doc. Wash: 5c.

CENTRAL AMERICA

General information relating to Central and South America, including a summary of consular rep'ts. 1912. Emigrants' information office, 34 Broadway, Westminster, S. W. Lond. 4d.

Jamaica, Panama canal, Central and South America. 1912. United fruit co. 17 Battery place, N. Y.

Latin American foreign trade in 1912. 1914. Pan Amer. union, Wash.

Map showing railroads of Latin America in operation and under construction, 16 by 21 inches. 1913. Pan Amer. union, Wash.

CEYLON

Ceylon, general information for intending settlers. 1912. Emigrants' information office, 34 Broadway, Westminster, S. W. Lond. 1d.

CHILE

Chile; an account of its wealth and progress by Julia P. Canto. 1912. Distributed by Pan Amer. union, Wash.

Chile; general descriptive data. 1913. Pan Amer. union, Wash.

Chile, its position, resources, climate, mining, fruit growing and farming by Chile-Foreign office. n. d. Distributed by the Pan Amer. union, Wash.

Commerce of Chile. (annual) Pan Amer. union, Wash.

The great nitrate fields of Chile. 1909. Pan Amer. union, Wash.

Opportunities for foreign trade in Chile by Chile-Foreign office. 1913. Distributed by Pan Amer. union, Wash.

Santiago de Chile. 1909. Pan Amer. union, Wash.

Views of the Chilean nitrate works and ports. n. d. Chilean nitrate propaganda, 25 Madison ave. N. Y.

CHINA

China. n. d. Canadian Pacific R. R. co. Pacific S. S. lines, Montreal, Canada.

Some roads towards peace by Charles W. Eliot. 1914. Carnegie endowment for international peace, 2 Jackson place, Wash.

COLOMBIA

Colombia; general descriptive data. 1913. Pan Amer. union, Wash.

Commerce of Colombia. (annual) Pan Amer. union, Wash.

COLORADO

Around the circle. c1907. Denver and Rio Grande R. R. Chic.

Colorado. n. d. Burlington route, Chic. Also other publications.

Colorado. n. d. Denver, northwestern and Pacific R. R. Denver.

Colorado, America's roof garden. n. d. Missouri Pacific-Iron Mountain R. R. St Louis, Mo.

Colorado climatology by R. E. Tremble. 1912. Bull. 182. Agricultural experiment station, Fort Collins.

Colorado for the tourist. 1913. Union Pacific R. R. Omaha, Neb. Also other publications.

A Colorado summer. 1913. Santa Fe, 1119 Railway exchange, Chic. Also other publications.

Denver to-day; descriptive, statistical, pictorial. 1914. Chamber of commerce, Denver.

Fertile lands of Colorado and northern New Mexico. c1909. Denver and Rio Grande R. R. Chic.

Map of Colorado showing all railroads, 56 by 44 cm. n. d. Railroad commission, Denver.

Picturesque Colorado. 1911. Colorado and southern R. R. Denver.

Thru the Rockies. n. d. Colorado midland R. R. Denver.

Tourists' handbook. (latest ed.) Denver and Rio Grande R. R. Chic.

Under the turquoise sky. c1910. Rock Island lines, Chic. Also other publications.

With nature in Colorado. n. d. Denver and Rio Grande R. R. Chic.

Colorado, see also Mesa Verde national park.

CONNECTICUT

Connecticut, industrial, agricultural, historical, and other facts concerning a progressive state. 1914. State board of trade. Board of trade, Hartford.

Made in Hartford; handbook and reports of the Board of trade. 1912. Board of trade, Hartford.

New Haven, Conn. n. d. Chamber of commerce, New Haven.

COSTA RICA

Commerce of Costa Rica. (annual) Pan Amer. union, Wash.

Commercial monograph of Costa Rica, no. 1. 1913. Dun's international review. Distributed by Pan Amer. union, Wash.

Costa Rica; general descriptive data. 1913. Pan Amer. union, Wash.

CRATER LAKE NATIONAL PARK

General information regarding Crater lake national park. (annual) Interior dep't, Wash.

Geological history of Crater lake. 1912. Interior dep't, Wash. or, Sup't of doc. Wash. 10c.

Panoramic view of Crater lake national park by J. H. Renshawe. 1914. Geological survey, Wash. 25c. or, Sup't of doc. Wash. 25c. 16½ by 18 inches; scale 1 mile to the inch.

CUBA

Commerce of Cuba. (annual) Pan Amer. union, Wash.

Cuba, a pamphlet descriptive of the island of Cuba. 1910. Dep't of agric. Havana.

Cuba; general descriptive data. 1913. Pan Amer. union, Wash.

A few facts and figures in regard to Cuba by Cuba—Dep't of agric. n. d. Distributed by Pan Amer. union, Wash.

Future farming in Cuba by Forbes Lindsay. 1913. Pan Amer. union, Wash.

La republique de Cuba. n. d. Distributed by Pan Amer. union,
Wash.

In French and English.

A winter paradise. c1912. United R. R. of Havana, 52 Broadway, N. Y.

DELAWARE

Delaware the diamond state. 1911. State board of agric. Dover.

Wilmington as a manufacturing center. 1911. Board of trade,
Wilmington.

DENMARK

Copenhagen and its environs. n. d. Published by the Danish
tourists' ass'n. Address Thos. Cook and son, 245 Broadway,
N. Y.

Notes on agricultural conditions in Denmark. 1913. 62nd cong.
3rd sess. Senate doc. 992. Wash. or, Sup't of doc. Wash.
5c.

DISTRICT OF COLUMBIA

Guide to the national capital. 1912. Pennsylvania lines, Pittsburgh, Penn.

The new Washington by George H. Gall. c1913. Chamber of
commerce, Wash.

Washington, old and new by Barry Bulkley. c1913. Distributed
by G. F. Schutt, The new Ebbitt, Wash.

DOMINICAN REPUBLIC

Commerce of the Dominican Republic. (annual) Pan Amer.
union, Wash.

Development of Dominican Republic by Charles H. Albrecht
and Frank A. Henry. 1914. Special consular rep't 65. Foreign and domestic commerce bur. Wash. or, Sup't of doc.
Wash. 5c.

Dominican Republic; general descriptive data. 1913. Pan Amer.
union, Wash.

Santo Domingo. (latest ed.) Clyde S. S. co. Pier 36, North
River, N. Y. Also other publications.

THE EAST (U. S.)

Mountain and lake resorts. 1913. Lackawanna R. R. 90 West
st. N. Y. 10c. Also other publications.

Summer excursion book. 1913. Pennsylvania R. R. N. Y.

East Africa, see Africa, East.

ECUADOR

Commerce of Ecuador. (annual) Pan Amer. union, Wash.

Ecuador; general descriptive data. 1913. Pan Amer. union, Wash.

EGYPT

Mediterranean cruises. 1913. Royal mail steam packet co. Address Thos. Cook and son, 245 Broadway, N. Y.

To the Levant and the land of the Pharaohs. n. d. North German Lloyd S. S. co. 5 Broadway, N. Y. Available.

ENGLAND

Cathedral route from London. 1913. Great eastern R. R. of England, 261 Broadway, N. Y. Available.

The Garden of England and the home of Dickens. 1912. Southeastern and Chatham R. R. of England, 334 Fifth ave. N. Y.

In the track of the Mayflower. n. d. London and southwestern R. R. 281 Fifth ave. N. Y. Also other publications.

The official guide to St Albans. (latest ed.) E. J. Burrow and co. ltd. Cheltenham, England. 3d.

Wonderful Wessex. 1913. Great western R. R. of England, 501 Fifth ave. N. Y. 20c. Also other publications. Available.

Federated Malay states, see Malay States, Federated.

FLORIDA

The everglades and other essays relating to southern Florida by John Gifford. c1912. Everglades sugar and land co. Miami.

Guide to Florida. (latest ed.) State bur. of information, Jacksonville.

Jacksonville. n. d. Distributed by Board of trade, Jacksonville. Also other publications.

Lee county, Florida; the borderland of the tropics. Board of county commissioners, Fort Myers, Florida.

Pictures and pointers about Pensacola. 1911. Commercial ass'n, Pensacola. Also publishes monthly bull. Greater Pensacola and other publications.

Semi-tropic Florida development year book. 1914. Tampa tribune, Tampa. 25c.

Southern Georgia and northern Florida. n. d. Georgia southern and Florida R. R. Macon, Ga.

Tampa, for health, wealth, and happiness. 1911-12. Board of trade, Tampa.

Wood using industries; the kudzu vine; citrus grove, its location and cultivation; pecan culture in Florida; cane grinding and syrup making. 1913. Dep't of agric. Tallahassee.

FRANCE

Pyrenees and Basque coast. French state railways bur. 2 Rector st. N. Y. Also other publications. Available.

The valley of the Rhone. n. d. Paris, Lyon. Méditerranée R. R. 281 Fifth ave. N. Y. Also other publications.

GENERAL GRANT NATIONAL PARK

General information regarding Sequoia and General Grant national parks. (annual) Interior dep't, Wash.

GEORGIA

Advantages of Georgia. (latest ed.) Dep't of agric. Atlanta.

Atlanta. n. d. Chamber of commerce, Atlanta. Also other publications.

Georgia. n. d. Southern R. R. Wash.

Savannah, municipal, financial, commercial, industrial, agricultural, residential, and historical. 1911. Chamber of commerce, Savannah.

Southern Georgia and northern Florida. n. d. Georgia southern and Florida R. R., Macon.

GERMANY

Economic conditions in Germany by J. G. Schmidlapp. 1914. Senate doc. 367. 63rd cong. 2nd sess. or, Sup't of doc. Wash. 5c.

GLACIER NATIONAL PARK

General information regarding Glacier national park. (annual) Interior dep't, Wash.

Glacier national park. n. d. Great northern R. R. St. Paul, Minn. Three other booklets 4c. each.

Glaciers of Glacier national park by W. C. Alden. 1914. Interior dep't, Wash. or, Sup't of doc. Wash. 15c.

Origin of scenic features of Glacier national park by Marius R. Campbell. 1914. Interior dep't, Wash. or, Sup't of doc. Wash. 15c.

Panoramic view of Glacier national park prepared by John H. Renshawe. 1914. Geological survey, Wash. or, Sup't of doc. Wash. 25c.

21 by 23 inches. Scale 3 miles to the inch.

Some lakes of Glacier national park. 1912. Interior dep't, Wash.
or, Sup't of doc. Wash. 10c.

Topographic map of Glacier national park. Geological survey,
Wash. 30c.

Size 32 by 28½ inches. Scale 2 miles to the inch.

GRAND CANYON OF THE COLORADO

Titan of chasms. n. d. Santa Fe R. R. 1119 Railway exchange.
Chic.

GUATEMALA

Commerce of Guatemala. (annual) Pan Amer. union, Wash.

Guatemala; general descriptive data. 1913. Pan Amer. union,
Wash.

Map of Guatemala by Guatemalan central R. R. lines. n. d. Distributed by Pan Amer. union, Wash.

HAITI

Commerce of Haiti. (annual) Pan Amer. union, Wash.

Haiti; general descriptive data. 1913. Pan Amer. union, Wash.

HAWAII

Annual rep't. (latest ed.) Honolulu chamber of commerce, Honolulu.

Commerce and industries of Alaska, Hawaii, Porto Rico, and the
Philippine Islands. 1913. Special agents ser. 67, Bur. of
foreign and domestic commerce, Wash. or, Sup't of doc.
Wash. 10c.

Hawaii by F. H. Newell. 1909. 60th cong. 2nd sess. Senate doc.
668. Wash. or, Sup't of doc. Wash. 10c.

Rep't of governor. 1912. Dep't of the interior, Wash. or, Sup't
of doc. Wash. 20c.

Rep't on Hawaii. 1910. Bur. of labor, Wash. or, Sup't of doc.
Wash. 30c.

Published every five years.

Holland, see Netherlands.

HONDURAS

Commerce of Honduras. (annual) Pan Amer. union, Wash.

Honduras; general descriptive data. 1913. Pan Amer. union,
Wash.

HUNGARY

The South railway in Austria-Hungary. n. d. published by the

South R. R. Vienna. Address Thos. Cook and son, 245 Broadway, N. Y.

The Trans-Danubian district, Croatia and the Hungarian coast. (latest ed.) Royal Hungarian state R. R. Address Thos. Cook and son, 245 Broadway, N. Y.

IDAHO

Boise, Idaho. n. d. Commercial club, Boise.

Eastern Washington and northern Idaho. n. d. Northern Pacific R. R. St Paul, Minn.

Great facts about a great region. n. d. Idaho-Washington development league, Lewiston.

Idaho, the dawn of plenty. 1912. 7th biennial rep't of Bur. of immigration, labor, and statistics, Boise.

Pacific northwest. 1910. Northwestern R. R. Chic.

Scenic Idaho. n. d. Oregon short line R. R. Salt Lake City, Utah. Also other publications.

The Twin Falls country, southern Idaho. n. d. Commercial club, Twin Falls. Also other publications.

Idaho, see also Yellowstone national park.

ILLINOIS

Chicago. n. d. Wabash R. R. Chic.

Chicago. c1912. Ass'n of commerce, 10 S. LaSalle st. Chic. 25c. (?) Also other publications.

Geography, history, and civics of Woodford county, Ill. Ed. by Roy L. Moore, County sup't of schools. Woodford county teachers' ass'n, Eureka.

The great middle west, the world's center of production and consumption; Peoria the central city. c1912. Ass'n of commerce, Peoria. 25c. Also other publications.

Greater Springfield. 1912. Commercial ass'n, Springfield.

Hamilton, Illinois. n. d. Wabash R. R. Chic.

Quincy. n. d. Chamber of commerce, Quincy. Also other publications.

Rockford. 1912. Chamber of commerce, Rockford. Also other publications.

INDIANA

Fort Wayne; a presentation of her resources, achievements, and possibilities. 1913. Commercial club, Fort Wayne.

Gary. n. d. Commercial club, Gary. 15c.

Official program and souvenir; encampment Indiana dep't Grand
army of the republic. 1912. Distributed by Chamber of
commerce, South Bend.
Contains description and illustration of the town.

IOWA

Davenport. Iowa; a city in which to live. n. d. Greater Davenport committee. 10c. Also other publications.
Des Moines, the city of certainties. n. d. Greater Des Moines
committee, Des Moines.

IRELAND

Southern Ireland; its lakes and landscapes. (latest ed.) Great
western R. R. of England, 501 Fifth ave., N. Y. 10c. Available.

ITALY

How to ascend Vesuvius. n. d. Thos. Cook and son, 245 Broadway, N. Y.
How to see Italy. n. d. North German Lloyd S. S. co. 5 Broadway, N. Y. Available.
The Italian lemon industry by G. H. Powell and F. O. Wallschlaeger. 1913. Bull. 10, Citrus protective league of California, Los Angeles, Cal.
Italy. n. d. Italian state R. R. 281 Fifth ave. N. Y. Available.
Mediterranean cruises. n. d. White star line, 9 Broadway,
N. Y. Available.

JAPAN

Japan. n. d. Canadian Pacific R. R. co. Pacific S. S. lines,
Montreal, Can.
Japanese characteristics by Charles W. Eliot. 1913· No. 71.
Amer. ass'n for international conciliation, 407 W. 117th st.
N. Y.
The rural life of Japan. 1910. Bur. for local affairs, Home dep't,
Tokyo, Japan.
Some roads towards peace by Charles W. Eliot. 1914. Carnegie
endowment for international peace, 2 Jackson place, Wash.

KANSAS

Biennial rep't. (latest ed.) State dep't of agric. Topeka.
Kansas, a small story of a great state. n. d. Santa Fe, 1119 Railway exchange, Chic.

Kansas, resources, population, industries, opportunities, and climate. 1909. Union Pacific R. R., Omaha, Neb.

Kansas, the bountiful. 1912. Rock Island-Frisco lines. Chic.

Kansas City is a manufacturing city. n. d. Commercial club, Kansas City.

Some of the publications of the Commercial club include material on Kansas City, Missouri, and Kansas City, Kansas.

Wichita the city of opportunities. n. d. Business ass'n, Wichita. Also other publications.

KENTUCKY

Kentucky. n. d. Southern R. R., Wash.

Louisville today. n. d. Commercial club, Louisville.

LOUISIANA

Agricultural resources and possibilities of Louisiana. n. d. Southern Pacific R. R. New Orleans.

Handbook of Louisiana. 1912. State board of agric. and immigration, Baton Rouge. Also other publications.

Louisiana. n. d. Joint immigration bur. 207 Missouri Pacific bldg, St Louis, Mo.

Louisiana, everyman's land. 1910. Rock Island lines. Chic.

Louisiana, nature's garden spot. n. d. Industrial and immigration commissioner, Ill. central R. R. Chic. Also other publications.

Map of Louisiana. 1913. Apply Dep't agric. and immigration, Baton Rouge.

A phyto-geographic map showing principal vegetation areas, all principal commercial points, town population and railway distances.

New Orleans for the tourist. 1909. Ill. central R. R. Chic.

New Orleans, what to see and how to see it. n. d. Ass'n of commerce, New Orleans. Also other publications.

Northwest Louisiana. n. d. Kansas City southern R. R. Kansas City, Mo.

On to Dixie. n. d. Cotton belt route, St Louis, Mo.

The wet lands of southern Louisiana and their drainage by Charles W. Okey. Dep't bull. 71, Agric. dep't, Wash. or, Sup't of doc. Wash. 15c.

Winter in New Orleans. 1912. Southern Pacific R. R. New Orleans.

MAINE

In the Maine woods. (latest ed.) Bangor and Aroostook R. R. Bangor. 15c.

Tourists' handbook of Portland, Maine. c1912. Board of trade, Portland.

MALAY STATES, FEDERATED

Federated Malay States, with a chapter on the Straits Settlements. 1912. Emmigrants' information office, 34 Broadway, Westminster, S. W. Lond. 6d.

Mining in the Federated Malay States by D. C. Alexander, jr 1912. Special agents ser. 59. Bur. of manufactures, Wash. or, Sup't of doc. Wash. 5c.

MANITOBA

Manitoba a forest province by R. H. Campbell. 1913. Circ. 7. Forestry branch, Ottawa, Can.

Nibigami (country of lakes). n. d. Grand trunk Pacific, Montreal, Can.

MARYLAND

The Baltimore book. c1914. Address Wilbur F. Coyle, City library, City hall, Baltimore.

Maryland, annual rep't. (latest ed.) Bur. of statistics and information, 100 Equitable bldg, Baltimore.

State of Maryland. (latest ed.) Board of public works, Baltimore.

MASSACHUSETTS

Boston, a guide book. 1912. Chamber of commerce, Bost. 10c.

Boston as a manufacturing center. n. d. Publicity and information bur. Bost. Also publishes a large map of Boston.

Boston's story in inscriptions. n. d. Worcester slipper co. Worcester.

Buzzard's bay. n. d. New York, New Haven, and Hartford R. R. Bost. Also other publications.

Progressive Springfield. c1914. George S. Graves, 21 Besse place, Springfield. 10c. Also other publications.

MESA VERDE NATIONAL PARK

Antiquities of the Mesa Verde national park; cliff palace by J. W. Fewkes. 1911. Bull. 51. Bur. of Amer. ethnology, Wash. or, House doc. 991. 61st cong. 2nd sess. or, Sup't of doc. Wash. 45c.

Antiquities of the Mesa Verde national park; spruce tree house
by J. W. Fewkes. 1909. Bull. 41. Bur. of Amer. ethnology,
Wash. or, Sup't of doc. Wash. 40c.

General information regarding Mesa Verde national park. (annual) Interior dep't, Wash.

MEXICO

Commerce of Mexico. (annual) Pan Amer. union, Wash.

Facts and figures about Mexico. 1911. National railways of
Mexico, Chic. Available.

Mexico; general descriptive data. Special ed. 1914. Pan Amer.
union, Wash.

New commercial atlas map of Mexico published by Rand, Mc-
Nally co. Chic. 1914. Distributed by Pan Amer. union,
Wash.

MICHIGAN

Alpena, Michigan; a city and county of opportunities. n. d.
Chamber of commerce, Alpena. Also other publications.

The city beautiful, Detroit. n. d. Wabash R. R. Chic.

Detroit, a city of to-day. n. d. Convention and tourists' bur.
Detroit.

Detroit. 1913. Board of commerce, Detroit. Also other publications.

Facts about Battle Creek, Michigan. n. d. Post land co. Battle
Creek.

Facts about Michigan. 1913. Boyne City, Gaylord and Alpena
R. R. Boyne City.

Grand Rapids, beautiful, industrial, commercial. n. d. Board
of trade, Grand Rapids. Also other publications.

Grand Traverse region. n. d. Committee of 21, Traverse City.

Greater Saginaw. 1912. Saginaw daily news. Distributed by
Board of trade, Saginaw.

The lure of Kalamazoo. 1912. Commercial club, Kalamazoo.

Michigan, agricultural, horticultural, and industrial advantages.
1914. Bull. 3. Immigration commission, Lansing.

Michigan agriculture; its present status and wonderful possibilities by R. S. Shaw. 1914. Special bull. 70. Michigan
agric. experiment station, East Lansing.

Western Michigan. n. d. Western Michigan development bur.
Traverse City. Also other publications.

Where to go and what about Saulte Ste Marie. n. d. Soo business men's ass'n, Saulte Ste Marie. Also other publications.

MINNESOTA

A competence from 40 acres in northern Minnesota. n. d. Soo line, Minn.

Duluth. 1913. Commercial club, Duluth. Also other publications.

Map of Minnesota. 1914. State auditor, St Paul. Also other publications.

Contains descriptive material on back.

Minneapolis, the city of lakes and gardens. n. d. Civic and commerce ass'n, Minn. Also other publications.

Minnesota. n. d. Great northern R. R. St Paul. Also other publications.

Minnesota. (latest ed.) Northern Pacific R. R. St Paul.

Minnesota, a land of opportunity. n. d. State board of immigration, St Paul. Also other publications.

Minnesota, the state of opportunities. 1912. Minn. state agric. society, Hamline.

Saint Paul, the gateway to the great northwest. n. d. Ass'n of commerce, St Paul. Also other publications.

MISSISSIPPI.

Jackson, Mississippi. 1913. Board of trade, Jackson. Also other publications.

Mississippi. 1912. Southern R. R. Wash.

Mississippi, a wonderful agricultural state. n. d. Industrial and immigration commissioner, Ill. central R. R. Chic. Also other publications.

Share Mississippi's opportunities. 1913. Dep't of agric. Jackson.

MISSOURI

Between trains in Kansas City. n. d . Commercial club of Kansas City. Also other publications.

Some of the publications of the commercial club include material on Kansas City, Missouri and Kansas City, Kansas.

Geography of Missouri. 1912. Missouri univ. bull. Educ. ser. v. 1, no. 4. Univ. of Missouri, Columbia.

Industrial information, labor resources, advantages, opportunities. 1912. Bur. of labor statistics, Jefferson City. Also other publications.

Jefferson City, Missouri. n. d. Distributed by Commercial club, Jefferson City. Also other publications.

Joplin, Missouri. 1913. Commercial club, Joplin. Also other publications.

Missouri. 1911. Rock Island lines, Chic.

Missouri and Arkansas Ozarks. n. d. Frisco lines, St Louis.

Municipal institutions of St Louis, where to go and what to see. 1914. City plan commission, St Louis.

The Ozark mountain region. n. d. Kansas City southern R. R. Kansas City, Mo.

St Joseph. n. d. Commerce club, St Joseph. Also other publications.

Southeast Missouri valley and ridge. n. d. Cotton belt route, St Louis.

Special Saint Louis number. Agents' bull. v. 6, no. 9, Nov. 1913. Missouri Pacific-Iron Mountain R. R. St Louis.

Trade and commerce of St Louis (latest rep't) Merchant's exchange, St Louis.

Gives description of industries and statistics.

Vacation days in St Louis. n. d. Business men's league, St Louis. Also other publications.

MONTANA

Butte, the wonder city of the west. 1912. Chamber of commerce, Butte.

The Deer Lodge valley. n. d. Chic. Milwaukee and St Paul R. R. Chic. Also other publications.

Great Falls leader; development edition. v. 26, no. 25. 1913. Leader co. Great Falls. 25c.

Montana. 1912. Bur. of agric. labor, and industry. Helena.

Montana, the treasure state. n. d. Great northern R. R. St Paul.

Montana, the treasure state. 1912. Northern Pacific R. R. St Paul. Not the same as preceding entry.

The resources and opportunities of Montana. 1914. Dep't of agric. and publicity, Helena.

Western Montana. 1913. Distributed by Chamber of commerce, Missoula.

Montana, see also Glacier national park, Yellowstone national park.

Mount Rainier National Park

General information regarding Mount Rainier national park. (annual) Interior dep't, Wash.

Mount Rainier and its glaciers by F. E. Matthes. 1914. Interior dep't, Wash. or, Sup't of doc. Wash. 15c.

The mountain of the great snow. n. d. Chic. Milwaukee and St Paul R. R. (Puget Sound lines), Seattle, Wash.

Nebraska

Beautiful Lincoln, Nebraska's capital city. n. d. Commercial club, Lincoln. Also other publications.

Nebraska, resources, population, industries, opportunities, and climate. 1909. Union Pacific R. R. Omaha.

Omaha, the best city of its size in the United States. n. d. Commercial club, Omaha. Also other publications.

Resources of Nebraska. 1913. Bull. 27. State bur. of labor and industrial statistics, Lincoln.

Western Nebraska. (latest ed.) Bur. of statistics, Lincoln.

Netherlands

Holland, the home of peace. c1913. Holland-America line, 39 Broadway, N. Y. Also other publications.

Through Holland. n. d. Netherland state R. R. and Flushing royal mail route, 334 Fifth ave. N. Y. Also other publications.

Nevada

Agricultural Nevada. n. d. Dep't of industry, agric. and irrigation. Carson City. Also other publications.

New Brunswick

New Brunswick. 1912. Interior dep't, Ottawa, Can.

St John, the city of the loyalists. 1913. Canadian government R. R. Halifax, Nova Scotia.

New England

Scenic and historic trips from Boston. Boston and Maine R. R. Bost.

New Hampshire

City of Manchester. c1912. Chamber of commerce, Manchester.

Concord, the capital of New Hampshire. 1909. Commercial club, Concord.

New Hampshire farms for summer homes. (latest ed.) State board of agric. Concord.

White mountains of New Hampshire. c1912. Boston and Maine
R. R. Bost.

NEW JERSEY

Along the shore and in the foothills. n. d. New Jersey central,
Newark. 4c. Also other publications.

Industrial exposition. 1913. Board of trade, Elizabeth.

Newark in the public schools of Newark. 1911. Board of education, Newark.
Course of study on Newark.

NEW MEXICO

Albuquerque, New Mexico. 1912. Commerce club, Albuquerque.

Fertile lands of Colorado and northern New Mexico. c1907.
Denver and Rio Grande R. R. Chic.

Land of sunshine. (latest ed.) Bur. of immigration, Albuquerque. Also other publications.

New Mexico the land of sunshine. (latest ed.) Rock Island lines,
Chic.

New Mexico the sunshine state. n. d. Santa Fe, 1119 Railway
exchange, Chic. Also other publications.

Old-new Santa Fe and round about. n. d. Santa Fe, Topeka,
Kan.

Santa Fe, New Mexico; nature's leading sanitarium. n. d. Chamber of commerce, Santa Fe. Also other publications, including map of Santa Fe.

Tourists' handbook. (latest ed.) Denver and Rio Grande R. R.
Chic.

NEW SOUTH WALES

New South Wales. (annual) Emigrants' information office, 34
Broadway, Westminster, S. W. Lond. 1d.

NEW YORK

Above the clouds and old New York by H. Addington Bruce.
c1913. F. W. Woolworth co., Woolworth bldg, N. Y.
Printed for distribution to visitors, but sometimes sent by
mail.

Albany, N. Y. n. d. Chamber of commerce, Albany.

The Catskill mountains. 1913. Ulster and Delaware R. R.
Kingston.

The commercial development of Niagara, 1805-1913. 1913. Industrial agent, Niagara Falls.

Farms for sale or rent in New York. (latest ed.) Bur. of statistics and farm lands, Albany.

The heart of the empire state. c1913. Distributed by Chamber of commerce, Utica. Also other publications.

The Hudson river. n. d. N. Y. central lines, N. Y.

Niagara Falls. n. d. N. Y. central lines, N. Y. Also other publications.

Oswego, the industrial and commercial city. 1913. Oswego daily times, Oswego.

Preservation of Niagara falls. 1911. Doc. 246, 62nd cong. 2nd sess. or, Sup't of doc. Wash. 20c.

Queensborough, being a description and illustrated book of the borough of Queens. 1913. Chamber of commerce, Queensborough.

Rate of recession of Niagara falls by G. K. Gilbert. 1907. Bull. 306, Geological survey, Wash. or, Sup't of doc. Wash. 15c.

Rochester, N. Y. the city of varied industries. 1912. Chamber of commerce, Rochester. 5c. Also other publications.

The Woolworth building. 1913. Atlantic Terra Cotta co. 1170 Broadway, N. Y.

Yearbook (latest). Chamber of commerce, Syracuse. Contains statistics of city.

New Zealand

Information relative to the port of Wellington, N. Z. Yearbook 1913-14. Wellington harbour board, Wellington.

New Zealand. Dep't of tourist and health resorts. Wellington.

New Zealand handbook. (annual). Emigrants' information office, 34 Broadway, Westminster, S. W. Lond. 1d.

New Zealand, its resources, industries, and trade by H. D. Baker. 1912. Special consular rep't 57. Bur. of foreign and domestic commerce, Wash. or, Sup't of doc. Wash. 15c.

Newfoundland

Commerce and industries of Canada and Newfoundland by A. G. Robinson. 1913. Special agents' ser. 76. Foreign and domestic commerce bur. Wash. or, Sup't of doc. Wash. 10c.

Newfoundland. 1908. Emigrants' information office, 34 Broadway, Westminster, S. W. Lond. 1d.

Newfoundland and Labrador. n. d. Reid Newfoundland co. St John's.

NICARAGUA

Commerce of Nicaragua. (annual) Pan Amer. union, Wash.

Nicaragua; general descriptive data. 1913. Pan Amer. union, Wash.

NORTH CAROLINA

Asheville, America's beauty spot. n. d. Board of trade, Asheville.

Charlotte, North Carolina. 1913. Greater Charlotte club, Charlotte.

Cotton culture in North Carolina. 1912. Dep't of agric, Raleigh.

A day in Raleigh. n. d. Chamber of commerce, Raleigh. Also other publications.

The land of the sky. n. d . Southern R. R. Wash. Also other publications.

Sketch of North Carolina. (latest ed.) Dep't of agric. Raleigh.

Some facts and figures about North Carolina and her natural resources. 1913. Geological survey, Raleigh.

Winston-Salem, city of industry. 1914. Board of trade, Winston-Salem. Also other publications.

NORTH DAKOTA

Bismarck and Burleigh county. n. d. Distributed by Commercial club, Bismarck. Also other publications.

Facts about Grand Forks. n. d. Commercial club, Grand Forks. Also other publications.

Fargo, the gateway to North Dakota. n. d. Commercial club, Fargo.

North Dakota. n. d. Great northern R. R. St Paul, Minn.

North Dakota and her magnificent resources. n. d. Dep't of agric. Bismarck.

Physiography of the Devil's-Stump lake region, N. D. by Howard E. Simpson in State geological survey. Biennial rep't, v. 6, 1912. State geological survey, Bismarck.

Western North Dakota. n. d. Northern Pacific R. R. St Paul, Minn.

What North Dakota offers. n. d. Soo line, Minn.

THE NORTHWEST

Along the scenic highway. n. d. Northern Pacific R. R. St Paul, Minn. Also other publications.

The land that lures, summer in the Pacific northwest. (latest ed.) Oregon-Washington R. R. and navigation co. Portland, Ore.

North Pacific coast country. 1907. Chic. Milwaukee and St Paul
R. R. Chic.

THE NORTHWEST, CANADIAN

Canada west, the last best west. 1913. Interior dep't, Ottawa,
Canada. Also other publications.

The western provinces of Canada. n. d. Canadian Pacific R. R.
Calgary, Alberta.

NORWAY

Norway, nature's wonderland. n. d. Norwegian America line,
8-10 Bridge st. N. Y. Also other publications.

To the midnight sun. c1913. Hamberg Amer. line, 41-45 Broadway, N. Y.

NOVA SCOTIA

Nova Scotia. 1912. Interior dep't, Ottawa, Can.

Storied Halifax. 1913. Canadian government R. R. Halifax.

NYASALAND

Nyasaland protectorate. 1911. Emigrants' information office, 34
Broadway, Westminster, S. W. Lond. 6d.

OHIO

Akron, the city of opportunity. n. d. Chamber of commerce,
Akron.

Cincinnati an old city made new. c1913. Chamber of commerce,
Cincinnati. Also other publications.

Columbus, Ohio. n. d. Board of trade, Columbus.

Toledo for transportation. 1913. Commerce club, Toledo.

OKLAHOMA

Agricultural resources of eastern Oklahoma. n. d. Eastern Oklahoma agric. ass'n, Barnes bldg, Muskogee.

Eastern Oklahoma. n. d. Kansas City southern R. R. Kansas
City, Mo.

The good state of Oklahoma. n. d. Santa Fe, 1119 Railway exchange, Chic.

Greater Muskogee. 1914. Commercial club, Muskogee. Also
other publications.

This is a monthly magazine but numbers are sent on request.

Guthrie, the manufacturing center of Oklahoma. n. d. Chamber
of commerce, Guthrie.

Oklahoma the twentieth century state. 1911. Rock Island lines, Chic.

The resources of Oklahoma in a pocket book by C. W. Shannon. 1912. Geological survey, Norman.

Tulsa; annual statement compiled by the auditing dep't, 1912-13. City auditor, Tulsa.

Gives material on commercial and industrial Tulsa.

ONTARIO

Hamilton, Canada; its history, commerce, industries, resources. 1913. City council. Hamilton; apply to H. M. Marsh, Commissioner of industries, Hamilton.

Improved Ontario farms for old country farmers. 1912. Interior dep't, Ottawa. Also other publications.

Ottawa, Canada. 1912. Publicity and industrial bur. Ottawa.

Rep't. (annual) Bur. of mines, Toronto.

   v. 21, pt 1, 1912, contains article on Mines of Ontario.

   v. 21, pt 2, 1912. Rep'ts on the district of Patricia, recently added to the province of Ontario.

Toronto, a city of opportunities. 1912. Toronto harbor commissioners, Toronto.

OREGON

Astoria and Clatsop county, Oregon. n. d. Chamber of commerce, Astoria.

Creswell, Oregon. n. d. Creswell development league, Creswell.

The economic geological resources of Oregon. 1912. State bur. of mines, Corvallis.

The mineral resources of Oregon, monthly. Oregon bur. of mines and geology, Corvallis.

Morrow county, Oregon. n. d. Morrow county booster club, Heppner.

Oregon. n. d. Great northern R. R. St Paul, Minn.

Oregon for the homeseeker. n. d. Northern Pacific R. R. St Paul, Minn. Also other publications.

Oregon, the land of opportunity. c1911. Chamber of commerce, Portland. Also other publications.

Pacific northwest. 1910. Northwestern R. R. Chic.

Portland, Oregon. n. d. Oregon-Washington R. R. and navigation co. Portland. Also other publications.

Portland, Oregon. n. d. Soo line, Chic.

Salem, Oregon. n. d. Board of trade, Salem.

The state of Oregon, resources and opportunities. 1912. State immigration commission, Portland.

Sutherlin, Oregon. n. d. Commercial club, Sutherlin.

Tillanook county, Oregon. n. d. Southern Pacific R. R. Portland. Also other publications.

Oregon, see also Crater Lake national park.

PANAMA

Commerce of Panama. (annual) Pan Amer. union, Wash.

Panama; general descriptive data. 1913. Pan Amer. union, Wash.

Panama and the West Indies. n. d. Royal mail steam packet co. 22 State st. N. Y.

PARAGUAY

Commerce of Paraguay. (annual) Pan Amer. union, Wash.

Paraguay; general descriptive data. 1913. Pan Amer. union, Wash.

PENNSYLVANIA

Birds eye view map of Philadelphia. Merchants' and manufacers' ass'n, N. E. cor 13th and Market sts, Phil.

Consider Harrisburg, the heart of distribution. n. d. Chamber of commerce, Harrisburg.

Pennsylvania and its manifold activities. 1912. Permanent international ass'n of navigation congresses, Rooms 348, 351, The Bourse, Phil. Also other publications.

See Pittsburgh first. 1914. Chamber of commerce, Pittsburgh. Also other publications.

Where business centers. 1913. Pittsburgh industrial development commission, Pittsburgh. Also other publications.

PERU

Commerce of Peru. (annual) Pan Amer. union, Wash.

Peru; general descriptive data. 1913. Pan Amer. union, Wash.

PHILIPPINE ISLANDS

Commerce and industries of Alaska, Hawaii, Porto Rico, and the Philippine Islands. 1913. Special agents ser. 67. Bur. of foreign and domestic commerce, Wash. or, Sup't of doc. Wash. 10c.

Commercial geography; the materials of commerce for the Philippines by Hugo H. Miller. 1911. Bur. of educ. Manila.

Lumbering industry of Philippines by John R. Arnold. 1914.
Special agents ser. 88. Foreign and domestic commerce
bur. Wash. or, Sup't of doc. Wash. 5c.

Philippine coconut industry by O. W. Barrett. 1913. Bur. of
agric. Manila.

The Philippine Islands. 1913. Insular affairs bur. Wash. or,
Sup't of doc. Wash. 10c.

Porto Rico

Commerce and industries of Alaska, Hawaii, Porto Rico, and the
Philippine Islands. 1913. Special agents ser. 67. Bur. of
foreign and domestic commerce, Wash. or, Sup't of doc.
Wash. 10c.

Porto Rico, the island of enchantment. n. d. N. Y. and Porto
Rico S. S. co. 11 Broadway, N. Y.

Prince Edward Island

Prince Edward Island. 1912. Interior dep't, Ottawa, Can.

Prince Edward Island, the garden of the gulf. 1913. Canadian
government R. R. Halifax, Nova Scotia.

Quebec

Montreal. n. d. Business men's league, 1651 Notre Dame st.
Montreal.

Montreal for tourists. (latest ed.) Delaware and Hudson R. R.
N. Y.

Quebec, the ancient capital. 1913. Canadian government R. R.
Halifax, Nova Scotia.

Queensland

Queensland. (annual) Emigrants' information office, 34
Broadway, Westminster, S. W. Lond. 1d.

Russia

Russia, a handbook on commercial and industrial conditions by
John H. Snodgrass and others. 1913. Special consular re-
ports 61, Bur. of foreign and domestic commerce, Wash. or,
Sup't of doc. Wash. 50c.

Russian-America line. n. d. Russian-America line, 27 Broadway, N. Y.

Sahara Desert

The great Sahara, a hot desert by Marion Weller. 1912. v. 9,
no. 4. Bull. Northern Ill. state normal school, DeKalb, Ill.

SALVADOR

Commerce of Salvador. (annual) Pan Amer. union, Wash.

Salvador; general descriptive data. 1913. Pan Amer. union, Wash.

SCOTLAND

Scotland for the holidays. (latest ed.) London and northwestern R. R. Address Thos. Cook and son, 245 Broadway, N. Y.

Tours in Scotland. 1913. Thos. Cook and son, 245 Broadway, N. Y.

SEQUOIA NATIONAL PARK

General information regarding Sequoia and General Grant national parks. (annual) Interior dep't, Wash.

SOUTH AFRICA

Union of South Africa. (annual) Emigrants' information office, 34 Broadway, Westminster, S. W. Lond. 1d.

SOUTH AMERICA

Commercial traveler in South America. 1914. Pan Amer. union, Wash.

General information relating to Central and South America; including a summary of consular rep'ts. 1912. Emigrants' information office, 34 Broadway, Westminster, S. W. Lond. 4d.

Latin American foreign trade in 1912. 1914. Pan Amer. union, Wash.

Map showing railroads of Latin America in operation and under construction. 1913. Pan Amer. union, Wash.

Size 16 by 21 inches.

South America. 1912. Lamport and Holt line, 301 Produce exchange, N. Y.

South America as an export field by Otto Wilson. 1914. Special agents ser. 81. Bur. of foreign and domestic commerce, Wash. or, Sup't of doc. Wash. 25c.

Gives a brief description of the industrial and commercial geography of the different countries of South America.

South American meat industry by A. D. Melvin. 1914. (from U. S. agric. dep't Year book, 1913). Year book separate 629. Div. of publications, Dep't of agric. Wash. or, Sup't of doc. Wash. 5c.

World race for rich South American trade by C. L. Chandler.

1913. Senate doc. 208, 63rd cong. 1st. sess. or, Sup't of doc. **Wash.** 5c.

Bibliography

Publications on South America, brief review of information available to manufacturers and exporters in bulletins issued by the Bur. of foreign and domestic commerce. 1913. Miscellaneous ser. 12. Foreign and domestic commerce bur. Wash. or, Sup't of doc. Wash. 5c.

SOUTH AUSTRALIA

Official year book of South Australia. 1913. South Australian government, 85 Gracechurch st. Lond. E. C. Also other publications.

South Australia. (annual) Emigrants' information office, 34 Broadway, Westminster, S. W. Lond. 1d.

SOUTH CAROLINA

Charleston, South Carolina. n. d. Chamber of commerce, Charleston.

Handbook of South Carolina. (latest ed.) Dep't of agric. commerce, and industries, Columbia. Also other publications.

South Carolina. n. d. Southern R. R. Wash.

SOUTH DAKOTA

Black Hills, South Dakota. 1912. Northwestern R. R. Chic.

Mitchell, the corn palace of the world. n. d. Commercial club, Mitchell.

Sioux Falls. n. d. Commercial club, Sioux Falls.

South Dakota. (latest ed.) Dep't of immigration, Huron.

SPAIN

Glimpses of Spain and Morocco. c1910. North German Lloyd S. S. co. 5 Broadway, N. Y.

Tours in Spain and Morocco. n. d. Thos. Cook and son, 245 Broadway, N. Y.

Trips through Spain. French state railways bur. 2 Rector st. N. Y.

STRAITS SETTLEMENTS

Federated Malay States; with a chapter on the Straits Settlements. 1912. Emigrants' information office, 34 Broadway, Westminster, S. W. Lond. 6d.

SWEDEN

Tours in Sweden. n. d. Scandinavian-Amer. line, 1 Broadway, N. Y. Available.

SWITZERLAND

Switzerland. 1909. Swiss Federal R. R. 241 Fifth ave. N. Y. Also other publications. Available.

TASMANIA

Tasmania. (annual) Emigrants' information office, 34 Broadway, Westminster, S. W. Lond. 1d.

TENNESSEE

Chattanooga. n. d. Chamber of commerce, Chattanooga. Also other publications.

Facts about Tennessee. 1911. Dep't of agric. Nashville. Also other publications.

Knoxville, the exposition city. 1913. Distributed by Board of commerce, Knoxville. Also other publications.

Map of Tennessee. 1913. Dep't of agric. and bur. of immigration, Nashville.

  Showing agricultural resources, counties, railways, post offices, public highways, rivers, soil formation, location of coal, phosphate, copper, and other minerals.

Memphis district. n. d. Business men's club, Memphis. Also other publications.

Plant an industry in Nashville, Tennessee and watch it grow. n. d. Industrial bur. Nashville. Also other publications.

The resources of Tennessee. (quarterly) State geological survey, Nashville. 8c a year.

TEXAS

Beaumont, a gateway to the marts of the world. 1910. Chamber of commerce, Beaumont. Also other publications.

Coming south? n. d. Chamber of commerce, Austin. Also publishes Austin progress, monthly.

Dallas, the city of the hour. n. d. Chamber of commerce, Dallas. Also other publications.

East-Southeast Texas. Texas and New Orleans R. R. Houston.

El Paso, what it is and why. c1914. Chamber of commerce, El Paso.

Galveston. n. d. Missouri, Kansas and Texas lines, St Louis, Mo

Houston. n. d. Chamber of commerce, Houston.

Profitable products of east Texas. n. d. Cotton belt route, St Louis, Mo. Also other publications.

Southwest Texas. n. d. Sunset route, Houston. Also other publications.

Texas, a southwest empire. 1910. Rock Island lines, Chic.

Under sapphire skies in San Antonio, Texas. c1910. Missouri Pacific-Iron Mountain R. R. St Louis, Mo. Also other publications.

Where to go in Galveston. n. d. Commercial ass'n, Galveston. Also other publications.

UGANDA

Uganda protectorate. (latest ed.) Emigrants' information office, 34 Broadway, Westminster, S. W. Lond. 6d.

UNITED STATES

Agricultural opportunities. 7 pamphlets. 1912. Immigration bur. Wash. or, Sup't of doc. Wash. 5c each.
   "The seven pamphlets, taken together, cover the whole country, including Alaska and Hawaii."

Supplements to the Abstract of the thirteenth census of the United States, 1910. 1914. Census bur. Wash.
   These supplements give the statistics of each of the 48 states except Maine, and for the District of Columbia.

URUGUAY

Commerce of Uruguay. (annual) Pan Amer. union, Wash.

Uruguay; general descriptive data. 1913. Pan Amer. union, Wash.

UTAH

Biennial rep't. 1913. Utah conservation commission, Salt Lake City.

Glimpse of Utah. c1907. Denver and Rio Grande R. R. Chic.

Logan City by G. Merle Taylor. 1911. Commercial boosters' club. Logan. Also other publications.

Ogden canyon. n. d. Publicity bur. Ogden. Also other publications.

Resources of the state of Utah. 1911. Union Pacific R. R. Omaha, Neb. Also other publications.

Salt Lake City and the state of Utah. n. d. Commercial club publicity bur. Salt Lake City.

Tourists' handbook. (latest ed.) Denver and Rio Grande R. R. Chic.

VENEZUELA

Commerce of Venezuela. (annual) Pan Amer. union. Wash.

Venezuela; general descriptive data. 1913. Pan Amer. union, Wash.

VERMONT

Burlington on Lake Champlain. n. d. Merchants' ass'n, Burlington.

Vermont, the land of Green Mountains. Bur. of publicity, office of the Sec'y of state, Essex Junction. Also other publications.

VICTORIA

Victoria. (annual) Emigrants' information office, 34 Broadway, Westminster, S. W. Lond. 1d.

Victorian year book. (latest ed.) Government statist, Melbourne.

VIRGINIA

The beautiful caverns of Luray. Luray caverns corporation, Luray.

Country life in Virginia. 1912. Chesapeake and Ohio R. R. Richmond.

Handbook of Virginia. 1911. Dep't of agric. and immigration, Richmond.

Norfolk, Virginia. 1914. Industrial commission, Norfolk. Also other publications.

Richmond, Virginia, yesterday and to-day. 1914. Chamber of commerce, Richmond.

Scenes and places of interest along the Norfolk and Western R. R. n. d. Norfolk and Western R. R. Roanoke. Also other publications.

WALES

North Wales, the British Tyrol. (latest ed.) Great western R. R. of England. 501 Fifth ave. N. Y. 10c. Available.

WASHINGTON

Annual rep't. (latest) Port of Seattle commission, Seattle.

The beauties and wonders of Puget sound. n. d. International S. S. co. Colman dock, Seattle.

Centralia, the hub city of southwestern Washington. n. d. Commercial club, Centralia. Also other publications.

Climate of western part of Puget sound basin by E. J. Saunders.
1912. Soils bur. Wash. or, Sup't of doc. Wash. 5c.

Homeseekers' guide to the state of Washington by Harry F. Giles.
1914. Bur. of statistics and immigration, Olympia. Also
other publications.

Kennewick, Washington. n. d. Commercial club, Kennewick.

Olympia, a capital capital, industries, resources, attractions. n. d.
Chamber of commerce, Olympia. Also other publications.

Pacific northwest. 1910. Northwestern R. R. Chic.

Seattle, manufactures and commerce. n. d. Oregon-Washington R. R. and navigation co. Seattle. Also other publications.

Seattle, Washington. n. d. Exploitation and industrial bur.
New chamber of commerce, Seattle. Also other publications.

Snohomish, Washington. n. d. Commercial club, Snohomish.

Southwestern Washington. 1911. Northern Pacific R. R. St
Paul, Minn. Also other publications.

Spokane, 'midst nature's summer home. n. d. Chamber of commerce, Spokane. Also other publications.

Spokane, Washington. (latest ed.) Soo line, Chic. 4c.

Sunnyside, Washington. n. d. Chamber of commerce, Sunnyside.

The Tacoma primer. n. d. Commercial club and chamber of
commerce, Tacoma.

Walla Walla valley, Washington. n. d. Commercial club, Walla
Walla.

Washington. n. d. Great northern R. R. St Paul, Minn. Also
other publications.

Wenatchee, the gateway. c1910. Commercial club, Wenatchee.

Western Washington. n. d. Chic. Milwaukee and St Paul R. R.
Chic. Also other publications.

Yakima valley, Washington. n. d. Yakima commercial club,
North Yakima.

Washington, see also Mount Rainier national park.

THE WEST

Booklets and folders on Arizona, California, Utah, etc. Sunset
magazine information bur. San Francisco, Cal. Sent for
express charges.

West Africa, see Africa, West.

WEST INDIES

Panama and the West Indies. n. d. Royal mail steam packet co. 22 State st. N. Y.

West Indies. 1911. Emigrants' information office, 34 Broadway, Westminster, S. W. Lond. 6d.

WEST VIRGINIA

Agricultural resources and possibilities. (latest ed.) State board of agric. Charleston.

Illustrated and descriptive Charleston, West Virginia. n. d. Distributed by Chamber of commerce, Charleston. Also other publications.

The real Wheeling. 1913. Board of trade, Wheeling. Also other publications.

WESTERN AUSTRALIA

Western Australia. (annual) Emigrants' information office, 34 Broadway, Westminster, S. W. Lond. 1d.

WISCONSIN

Annual rep't (latest) Chamber of commerce, Milwaukee. 25c Gives statistics of trade and commerce.

Annual rep't of the city statistician of Superior, Wisconsin. 1912 City statistician, Superior.

The climate of Wisconsin and its relation to agriculture by A. R Whitson and O. E. Baker. 1912. Bull. 223. Agric. experiment station, Madison.

Commercial Milwaukee. 1914. Merchants' and manufacturers' ass'n, Milwaukee.

Garden of Eden. n. d. Soo line, Minn.

Geography and industries of Wisconsin by R. H. Whitbeck. 1913. Geological and natural history survey, Madison. Also other publications.

Greater Racine. 1911. Distributed by Commercial club, Racine.

North Wisconsin farm edition of the Superior telegram. Distributed by Commercial club, Superior. Also other publications.

Opportunities for profitable farming in northern Wisconsin by E. J. Delwiche. 1913. Bull. 196. Agric. experiment station Madison.

Wisconsin and its opportunities. n. d. Soo line, Minn.

Wisconsin opportunities. Commissioner of immigration, Madison. Also other publications.

WYOMING

The Big Horn basin. n. d. Burlington route, Chic.

The Cheyenne of to-day. n. d. Industrial club, Cheyenne.

Wonderful Wyoming. (latest ed.) State board of immigration, Cheyenne. Also other publications.

Wyoming and its attractions. n. d. Union Pacific R. R. Chic.

Wyoming, see also Yellowstone national park.

YELLOWSTONE NATIONAL PARK

The Cody road into Yellowstone park. n. d. Burlington route, Chic. Also other publications.

Fossil forests of the Yellowstone national park by F. H. Knowlton. 1914. Interior dep't, Wash. or, Sup't of doc. Wash. 10c.

General information regarding Yellowstone national park. (annual) Interior dep't, Wash.

Geological history of the Yellowstone national park. 1912. Interior dep't, Wash. or, Sup't of doc. Wash. 10c.

Map of Yellowstone national park. Sup't of doc. Wash. 40c. 28½ by 32 inches; scale 2 miles to the inch.

Through wonderland. Northern Pacific R. R. St Paul, Minn. 6c. Also other publications.

Where gush the geysers. c1913. Oregon short line, Chic.

Yellowstone national park. c1913. Northern Pacific R. R. St Paul, Minn. Also other publications.

Yellowstone national park. n. d. Chic. Milwaukee, and St Paul R. R. Chic.

YOSEMITE NATIONAL PARK

General information regarding Yosemite national park. (annual) Interior dep't, Wash.

Panoramic view of Yosemite national park prepared by J. H. Renshaw. 1914. Geological survey, Wash. 25c. or, Sup't of doc. Wash. 25c.

18½ by 18 inches; scale 3 miles to the inch. Other maps may be obtained from Sup't of doc. Wash. one 28½ by 27 inches; scale 2 miles to the inch. 50c; another 35 by 15½ inches; scale 2000 feet to the inch. 20c.

Sketch of Yosemite national park. 1912. Interior dep't, Wash. or, Sup't of doc. Wash. 10c.

INDUSTRIES AND COMMERCIAL PRODUCTS

ASPHALT

Trinidad and Bermudez asphalts and their use in highway construction by Clifford Richardson, reprinted from Popular science monthly, July-August, 1912. Distributed by Barber asphalt paving co. Phil. Also other publications.

BINDER TWINE

Binder twine industry. c1912. International harvester co. of New Jersey. Agric. extension dep't, Harvester bldg, Chic. 20c. Also other publications.

BOOKS

The biography of a book. n. d. Harper and brothers. N. Y.
The story of the making of a book. c1914. Charles Scribner's sons, N. Y.

BREAD

Story of bread. 1911. International harvester co. of New Jersey, inc. Agric. extension dep't, Harvester bldg, Chic. 3c.
Story of the staff of life. n. d. National ass'n of master bakers, Phil.

CARBORUNDUM

The man who didn't know when he had failed by F. W. Haskell. c1911. Carborundum co. Niagara Falls, N. Y. Also other publications.

CEMENT AND CONCRETE

Concrete construction about the home and on the farm. 1909. Atlas Portland cement co. N. Y. Also other publications.
Concrete pavements, sidewalks, curb, and gutter. c1913. Universal Portland cement co. 208 S. LaSalle st. Chic. Also other publications.

   To schools offering courses in agriculture a set of published lectures is supplied; charts and sets of lantern slides, illustrating the lectures, are loaned.
Handy cement book. (latest ed.) German-American Portland cement works. Chic. Also other publications.

CHINA

Book on china. Onondaga pottery co. Syracuse, N. Y.
The china book. c1912. Homer Laughlin china co. Newell, W. Va.

CHOCOLATE

Cocoa and chocolate. (latest ed.) Walter Baker and co. Dorchester, Mass. Also other publications.
Food of the gods; a handbook on cocoa and chocolate. Huyler's chocolate works, 18th st. and Irving place, N. Y.

COAL MINING

Coal mining practice in Danville, Ill. by S. O. Andros. 1914. Bull. 2 of Ill. coal mining investigation, Urbana, Ill. Also other publications.

COCOA

Cocoa. 1909. Pan Amer. union, Wash.
Cocoa and chocolate. (latest ed.) Walter Baker and co. Dorchester, Mass. Also other publications.
Cocoa production and trade. 1912. Special consular reports 50. Bur. of manufactures, Wash. or, Sup't of doc. Wash. 5c.
Food of the gods; a handbook on cocoa and chocolate. Huyler's chocolate works, 18th st. and Irving place, N. Y.

COCOANUT

The Philippine cocoanut industry by O. W. Barrett. 1913. Bull. 25. Bur. of agric. Manila, P. I.

COFFEE

Coffee. 1909. Pan Amer. union, Wash.
Coffee, production, trade, and consumption by countries, by H. C. Graham. 1912. Bull. 79 Bur. of statistics, Dep't of agric. Wash. or, Sup't of doc. Wash. 15c.

CORK

Cork; being the story of the origin of cork, the processes employed in its manufacture, its various uses in the world today. 1909. Armstrong cork co. Pittsburgh, Penn.

COTTON

Cotton. 1909. Pan Amer. union, Wash.
Cotton growing. (latest ed.) by D. A. Tompkins, Charlotte, N. C. Also other publications.

COTTON MANUFACTURE

City of Manchester, N. H. and the Amoskeag manufacturing co. c1912. Chamber of commerce, Manchester, N. H.
Contains pictures of cotton and woolen manufacturing.

FISHING

Preparation of the cod and other salt fish for the market by A. W. Bitting. 1911. Bull. 133. Bur. of chemistry, Wash. or, Sup't of doc. Wash. 15c.

FLAVORING EXTRACTS

Vanilla and other flavoring extracts. n. d. Joseph Burnett co. 36 India st. Bost.

FLAX

Hints for flax growers. 1911. Bull. 24. Dep't of agric. Regina, Saskatchewan.

FLOUR

Flour. (latest ed.) Pillsbury-Washburn flour mills co. Minn. Also other publications.
The miller's almanac. (annual) The northwestern miller, Minn. 50c.
Largely statistics.
Occident is no accident. c1909. Russell-Miller milling co. Minn.
The wheat and flour primer. c1910. Washburn-Crosby co. Minn.

HARVEST AND HARVESTING

Harvest scenes of the world. 1913. International harvester co. of New Jersey, inc. Agric. extension dep't, Harvester bldg, Chic. 50c.

HEMP

Hemp by Lyster H. Dewey. 1914. (from Dep't of agric. Yearbook 1913). Yearbook separate 628. Div. of publications, Dep't of agric. Wash. or, Sup't of doc. Wash. 15c.

INDUSTRIES

New England industries. n. d. Oxford print, 148 High st. Bost.

JUTE

Linen, jute and hemp industries in the United Kingdom by W. A. G. Clark. 1913. Special agents ser. 74. Bur. of foreign and domestic commerce, Wash. or, Sup't of doc. Wash. 25c.

KAPOK

The kapok industry by M. M. Saleeby. 1913. Bull. 26. Bur. of
agric. Manila, P. I.

LIMESTONE

Indiana limestone. n. d. Indiana limestone quarrymen's ass'n,
Bedford, Ind.

Will soon have for a loan a cinematographic film showing
each and every stage in the process of preparing Indiana
limestone ready to set building.

LINEN

Linen, jute and hemp industries in the United Kingdom by W. A.
G. Clark. 1913. Special agents ser. 74. Bur. of foreign and
domestic commerce, Wash. or, Sup't of doc. Wash. 25c.

LUMBER INDUSTRY

Annual report, 1911. National lumber manufacturers' ass'n,
1621 Otis bldg, Chic.

The pine cone, exposition number, May, 1914. The pine cone,
1014 Germania life bldg, St Paul, Minn.

Timber land bonds analyzed as investments. c1913. Clark L.
Poole and co. Chic.

Not intended for general distribution but libraries may possibly obtain copies.

Timber underwritings. n. d. Howard, Simmons and co. First
national bank bldg, Chic.

PACKING INDUSTRY

Armour products and packing methods. (latest ed.) Armour
co. Chic. Also other publications.

The evolution of a vast industry. (latest ed.) Swift and co.
Chic. Also other publications.

The pictorial history of a steer. c1909. Morris and co. Chic.
Also other publications.

PAPER

Crop plants for paper making by C. J. Brand. 1911. Circ. 82.
Bur. of plant industry, Wash. or, Sup't of doc. Wash. 5c.

PECAN

Opportunities in pecan culture by C. A. Reed. 1913. Circ. 112.
Bur. of plant industry, Wash. or, Sup't of doc. Wash. 10c.

Pecan and hickory in Texas by E. J. Kyle. Dep't of agric. Austin, Texas.

PENCILS

Pencil geography. c1904. Joseph Dixon crucible co. Jersey City, N. J.

PINEAPPLE.

Pineapple growing in Porto Rico by H. C. Hendricksen and M. J. Irons. 1909. Div. of publications, Dep't of agric. Wash. or, Sup't of doc. Wash. 15c.

PLATE GLASS

The making of plate glass. n. d. Pittsburgh plate glass co. Pittsburgh, Penn.

POTASH INDUSTRY

Potash industry. n. d. German Kali works, inc. McCormick bldg, Chic. Also other publications.

RICE

Rice and rice cookery by Miriam Birdseye. Cornell reading course, Jan. 1, 1914. Reprinted and distributed by The rice millers ass'n, room 209, Kyle bldg, Beaumont, Texas. Also other publications.

Rice culture in the Philippines. 1912. Bull. 22. Bur. of agric. Manila, P. I.

Rice growing the royal road to riches. 1910. Rock Island lines, Chic.

Rise of rice in Arkansas. n. d. Cotton belt route, St Louis, Mo.

Texas and Louisiana rice. n. d. Sunset route, Houston, Texas.

RUBBER

Rubber and its relatives. 1909. Pan Amer. union, Wash.

Rubber from forest to foot. c1913. United States rubber co. Broadway at 58th st, N. Y. Also other publications.

SALMON

Salmon data. 1913. Salmon canners ass'n, Seattle, Wash.

Salmon fisheries of the Pacific coast. 1911. Fisheries bur. Wash. or, Sup't of doc. Wash. 15c.

SHEARS

Pointed sharpness. n. d. J. Wiss and sons co. Newark, N. J.

SHIP BUILDING

Aquitania, the making of a mammoth liner by E. K. Chatterton.
n. d. Cunard steamship co. ltd, 21-24 State st, N. Y.

SHOES

Goodyear welt shoes. c1909. United shoe manufacturing co.
Bost.

A short history of American shoemaking by Fred A. Gannon.
c1912. Distributed by Sec'y, New England shoe and leather
ass'n, 166 Essex st, Bost. Also other publications.

SILK

A short description of silk and silk manufacture. n. d. Cheney
brothers, South Manchester, Conn.

Silk culture and manufacturing shown progressively. n. d.
Belding brothers, Rockville, Conn.

The silk industry, from the worm to the wearer. n. d. M. Heminway and sons silk co. 890 Broadway, N. Y.

Silk, its origin, culture and manufacture. 1911. Corticelli silk
mills, Florence, Mass. pap. 10c. cloth 24c.

SOAP

The Larkin idea; its home. Larkin co. Buffalo, N. Y.

SOUP

Franco-American soups; how they are made in a model establishment. c1909. Franco-American food co. Jersey City
Heights, N. J.

SUGAR

The American beet sugar industry in 1910 and 1911. 1912. Bull.
260. Bur. of plant industry, Wash. or, Sup't of doc. Wash.
25c.

Some interesting facts about sugar. 1912. Distributed by American sugar refining co. 117 Wall st. N. Y. Also other publications.

Sugar at a glance by T. G. Palmer. 1912. 62nd cong. 2nd sess.
Senate doc. 890. Wash. or, Sup't of doc. Wash. 15c.

Sugar cane and sirup making by A. P. Spencer. 1913. Bull.
118. Agric. experiment station, Gainesville, Fla.

Sugar industry, sugar cane and cane sugar in Louisiana. 1913.
Miscellaneous ser. 9. Foreign and domestic commerce bur.
Wash. or, Sup't of doc. Wash. 15c.

TAPIOCA

The story of tapioca. n. d. Minute tapioca co. Orange, Mass.

TEA

Cultivation and manufacture of tea in the United States by G. F. Mitchell. 1912. Bull. 234. Bur. of plant industry, Wash. or, Sup't of doc. Wash. 10c.

TOBACCO

Tobacco. 1909. Pan. Amer. union, Wash.

VANILLA

About vanilla. c1900. Joseph Burnett co. 36 India st. Bost.

WOOD USING INDUSTRIES

Wood using industries of California by A. K. Armstrong. 1912. State board of forestry, Sacramento, Calif.

Wood using industries of Iowa by H. Maxwell and J. T. Harris. 1913. Iowa state college of agric. Ames, Iowa.

Wood using industries of New Hampshire by R. E. Simmons. 1912. State forester, Concord, N. H.

Wood using industries of Ohio by C. W. Dunning. 1912. Ohio agric. experiment station, Wooster, Ohio.

Wood using industries of Ontario by R. G. Lewis and W. G. H. Boyce. 1913. Forestry branch, Ottawa, Can.

Wood using industries of South Carolina by Stanley L. Wolfe. 1913. Dep't of agric. commerce and industries, Columbia, S. C.

Wood using industries of Vermont by H. Maxwell. 1913. State board of agric. and forestry, Montpelier, Vt.

Wood using industries of Virginia by R. E. Simmons. 1912. Dep't of agric. and immigration, Richmond, Va.

WOOLEN MANUFACTURE

City of Manchester, N. H. and the Amoskeag manufacturing company. c1912. Chamber of commerce, Manchester, N. H. Contains pictures of cotton and woolen manufacturing.

From wool to cloth. c1911. Amer. woolen co. Bost.

MISCELLANEOUS

ANTARCTIC EXPLORATION

Expedition to South pole by Roald Amundsen. 1913. Publication 2224. Smithsonian institution, Wash.

BIG TREES

Big trees of California. Southern Pacific R. R. Chic.

Secret of the big trees, Yosemite, Sequoia, and General Grant national parks by Ellsworth Huntington. 1913. Interior dep't, Wash. or, Sup't of doc. Wash. 5c.

CLIMATE

Fluctuating climate of North America by Ellsworth Huntington. Publication 2206. Smithsonian institution, Wash.

CLOUDS

Description of cloud forms. 1913. Weather bur. Wash. or, Sup't of doc. Wash. 5c.

DOCKS

Rep't on physical characteristics of European seaports by C. W. Staniford. Dep't of docks and ferries, Pier A, North River, N. Y.

Seaport studies by Charles E. Fowler in University extension journal, v. 1, no. 1, Jan. 1914. Univ. of Wash. Seattle. Contains bibliography.

FROST

Notes on frost. Revised 1911. Farmers' bull. 104. Agric. dep't Wash. or, Sup't of doc. Wash. 5c.

GEYSERS

Geysers. 1912. Dep't of the interior, Wash. or, Sup't of doc. Wash. 10c.

IMPORTS AND EXPORTS

Trade of the United States with the world, 1912-13, imports and exports of merchandise into and from the United States by countries and principal articles. 1914. Miscellaneous ser. 15. Foreign and domestic commerce bur. or, Sup't of doc. Wash. 15c.

LEVEES

Great American levees by Haviland, Dozier, and Tibbetts. c1913. West Sacramento co. Sacramento, Calif.

METEOROLOGY

Brief list of meteorological textbooks and reference books by C. F. Talman. 1913. Ed. 3. Weather bur. Wash.

National Parks

"Collection of 83 photographs of national parks, in color, of a size to cover a 250-foot wall space in single tier." Loaned for exhibition purposes on payment of transportation charges. Office of the Secretary, Interior dep't, Wash.

Panama Canal

Panama canal guide book. 1913. Panama R. R. co. Colon, Canal Zone.

World race for the rich South American trade by C. L. Chandler. 1913. Senate doc. 208, 63rd cong. 1st. sess. or, Sup't of doc. Wash. 5c.

Panama canal and canal zone. Public documents for sale by Sup't of doc. 1914. Sup't of doc. Wash.

Panama-Pacific International Exposition

Information for visitors. c1913. Panama-Pacific international exposition, San Francisco, Calif. Also other publications.

Panama-Pacific international exposition. c1913. Remington typewriter co. 327 Broadway, N. Y.

Panama-Pacific international exposition. n. d. Santa Fe, 1119 Railway exchange, Chic.

Physical Geography

Course in meteorology and physical geography by W. N. Allen. 1911. Bull. 39. Weather bur. Wash. or, Sup't of doc. Wash. 20c.

Pictures

Report of the committee on instruction by means of pictures. 1913. School doc. no. 6, 1913. Boston public schools, Bost.

Time

Time taking, time keeping. n. d. Elgin national watch co. Elgin, Ill.

Trans-Siberian Railroad

Trans-Siberian R. R. and connections. 1913. International sleeping car co. 281 Fifth ave. N. Y.

Water Power

Electric power from the Mississippi, a description of the water-power development at Keokuk, Iowa. 1913. Mississippi river power co. Keokuk, Iowa.

WEATHER FORECASTS

Forecasting the weather by George S. Bliss. 1913. Bull. 42. Weather bur. Wash. or, Sup't of doc. Wash. 5c.

WINDS

Winds of the United States and their economic uses by P. C. Day, Weather bur. Wash. or, Sup't of doc. Wash. 5c.

THE WORLD

Atlas of the world. c1911. Cunard S. S. co. 21-24 State st. N. Y.

Diplomatic and consular reports. Annual ser. issued by the Foreign office of Great Britain. Obtain list from Wyman and sons, ltd. Fetter Lane, E. C. Lond. Price ranges from ½d.-6½d. each.

    Gives trade returns from practically all countries. Valuable series.

International map of the world. (Bost. including R. I. and portions of N. Y. Conn. Mass. N. H. Me. and N. S.) Sheet north K-19. Geological survey, Wash. or, Sup't of doc. Wash. 40c.

Other sheets have been issued as follows:

North 0-30. Scotland, The Highlands.

North 0-29. The Hebrides. (Europe).

North K-35. Instambul (Constantinople).

South H-34. Kenhardt (Africa). Address Edward Stanford, 12-14 Long Acre, W. C. Lond. 2s plus postage.

EDUCATIONAL EXHIBITS

This list has been compiled from answers to letters sent out to practically all of the American firms listed in the following bibliographies, as well as to others not listed. A few of the exhibits cost too much for small schools but are included to make the list useful to large schools.

Bibliography

Address list for illustrative materials and laboratory supplies for instruction in household arts. 1912. Technical educ. Bull. 12. Teachers' college, Columbia university, N. Y. 10c.

    Lists of exhibits. charts, booklets, etc., on foods, textile materials and fabrics.

Educational exhibits by Ellen B. McDonald in Normal instructor, 23·52, Dec. 1913.

Educational exhibits, in Delia G. Ovitz. Course in reference work and some bibliographies of special interest to teachers, p. 25. 1913. State normal school, Milwaukee, Wis. 10c.

Illustrative materials for geography by W. M. Gregory, in Journal of geography, 11:19-20, Sept. 1912. Same article with one addition in School news, 26:409, May, 1913.

Manufacturers' exhibits, in J. C. Dana. The school department room, p. 16. 1910. Elm tree press, Woodstock, Vermont. 35c.

ASBESTOS

H. W. Johns-Manville co. 201-231 Clybourn st. Milwaukee, Wis.

Samples of crude asbestos, asbestos fiber and finished product. Free.

Keasbey and Mattison co. Ambler, Pa.

Samples of crude asbestos, carded fiber and finished product. Free.

BAKING POWDER

Royal baking powder co. Royal bldg. William and Fulton sts. N. Y.

Illustrates the manufacture of cream of tartar. Free to schools in which domestic science is taught.

BUTTONS

German-American button co. Rochester, N. Y.

Exhibit showing vegetable ivory nut and the processes of manufacture of buttons. 50c.

CARBORUNDUM

Carborundum co. Niagara Falls, N. Y.

Samples of crude carborundum and of finished product. Free.

CEMENT (PORTLAND)

Atlas Portland cement co. 30 Broad st, N. Y.

Samples of raw material, clinker and finished product. Free.

German-American Portland cement works, 140 S. Dearborn st. Chic.

Four glass bottles showing the different stages in the manufacture of Portland cement. Free to schools and educational institutions.

CEREALS

Postum cereal co. ltd. Battle Creek, Mich.

Fourteen bottles showing the different stages in the process of manufacturing their products from wheat, corn, rice and barley. Free, charges prepaid.

COCOA AND CHOCOLATE

Walter Baker and co. ltd. Milton, Mass.
Free to schools.
Hershey chocolate co. Hershey, Penn.
Shows the process of cocoa manufacture from the bean in its natural state to the finished product. Free.
Huyler's, S. E. cor. 18th st, and Irving place, N. Y.
Free.
The Walter M. Lowney co. 486 Hanover st. Bost.
Showing cocoa from the raw bean to the finished product. Free.

COFFEE

C. F. Blanke tea and coffee co. 7th and Clark ave. St Louis, Mo.
About 25 bottles showing the various stages that coffee passes through from the time it leaves the plantation until it is ready for use; contains also samples of different varieties of tea. $3.00, freight collect.

CORK

Armstrong cork co. Pittsburgh, Penn.
Collection showing corkwood in various stages of manufacture. $1.00.

COTTON

Cambridge botanical supply co. Waverly, Mass.
Entire cotton plant, products of cotton seed, etc. $4.50.

COTTON, SPOOL

Spool cotton co. 315 Fourth ave. cor. 24th st. N. Y.
Limited number of spool cotton specimen cases, showing thread in various stages of manufacture. Free on application of principal.

FERTILIZERS

Swift and co. National stock yards, Ill.
Samples showing fertilizers made from by-products of the packing industry. Free.

FIBRE

International harvester co. of New Jersey. Agricultural extension dep't, Harvester bldg, Chic.

Consists of samples of sisal and manila fibre with small sample balls of twine and three booklets. 35c.

FLAX

Linen thread co. 96-98 Franklin st. cor. Church. N. Y.

Flax in different stages of manufacture from the raw material to the finished product. $3.00, express collect.

James McCutcheon and co. Fifth ave. at 34th st. N. Y.

Illustrates the various stages in the growth and manufacture of flax. Free to domestic departments of high schools and colleges; freight charges collect.

FLOUR

Hecker-Jones-Jewell milling co. Produce exchange, N. Y.

Furnished only to schools in New York state.

Pillsbury flour mills co. Minn.

Consists of twelve samples showing the different stages of flour manufacture. Free, express charges to be guaranteed by applicant; weight about 18 lbs.

Washburn-Crosby co. Minn.

Supply of exhibits temporarily exhausted. Free to schools or educational institutions.

GRAIN

Commissioner of immigration, Winnipeg, Can.

Samples of grain and grasses in straw and samples of threshed grain. Probably free.

GRINDING STONES

Pike manufacturing co. Littleton, N. H.

Shows the raw material and finished product. Free.

LIMESTONE

Indiana quarries co. 112 W. Adams st. Chic.

Samples of Bedford limestone. Free.

MILK, MALTED

Horlick's malted milk co. Racine, Wis.

Exhibit shows wheat, flour, barley and barley malt. Free.

NEEDLES

Spoon cotton co. 315 Fourth ave. cor 24th st. N. Y.

Limited number of needle specimen cases, showing needles in various stages of manufacture. Free on application of principal.

Nitrate Industry

Chilean nitrate propaganda, 25 Madison ave. N. Y.
Limited number of lantern slides for distribution, which show the stages in the Chilean nitrate industry.

Packing Industry

Armour and co. Chic.
Exhibit of by-products. $10.00.
Morris and co. Chicago.
Samples of tallow, glue fertilizers, showing by-products of packing industry. Free.

Paint and Varnish

Sherwin-Williams co. 601 Canal road N. W. Cleveland, Ohio.
Shows raw material. Probably free.

Pencils

Joseph Dixon crucible co. 501 Victoria bldg, St Louis, Mo.
From crude graphite and cedar strips to the finished product. Free to schools.
Eberhard Faber, 37 Greenpoint ave. Brooklyn, N. Y.
Steps in the manufacture of a pencil from crude graphite and cedar strip to the finished product. Free.

Pens

Esterbrook steel pen mfg co. Camden, N. J.
Shows by samples the steps in the manufacture of pens from the sheet steel to the finished product. 10c.
Spencerian pen co. 349 Broadway, N. Y.
25c.

Petroleum

Standard oil co. 72 West Adams st. Chic.
Samples of 21 petroleum products. Distributed only to large schools.

Potash

German Kali works. 1901 McCormick bldg, Chic.
Sent only to institutions in which agriculture is taught.

RUBBER

United States Rubber co. Broadway at 58th st. N. Y.
$10.00.

SALT.

Diamond crystal salt co. St Clair, Mich.

Contains samples of crude salt and of salt in different stages of manufacture. Free to schools on payment of express charges; in middle west charges amount to about 75c.

Worcester salt co. 71-73 Murray st. N. Y.

Samples of salt. Free to schools.

SHEARS

J. Wiss and sons co. Newark, N. J.

Shows steps in the manufacture of shears. Free, express collect; in middle west charges amount to between 20 and 30c.

SILK

Belding bros. and co. 201 West Monroe st. Chic.

Silk exhibit. $1.25.

Corticelli silk mills, Florence, Mass.

Box of two cocoons, 5c; silk culture chart, 20c; silk culture cabinet, $1.25 if intended for educational exhibit in schools.

M. Heminway and sons silk co. 890 Broadway, N. Y.

Samples of silk cocoons, raw silk and silks in process of manufacture. Free, express charges collect; in the middle west the charges amount to between 30 and 40c.

T. A. Keleher, P. O. box 3203, Sta. F, Wash. D. C.

Silk cocoon exhibit, 15c; other more comprehensive exhibits ranging in price from 50c to $1.00.

SOAP

Larkin co. Buffalo, N. Y.

Bottles showing ingredients of soap, its appearance at different stages and the finished product. Free, express charges collect; in the middle west the charges will amount to between 40 and 50c.

SPICES

McCormick and co. Baltimore, Md.

Soon to have for distribution a set of color plates showing the different varieties of commercial spices in various stages of their growth. Free.

STEEL

Illinois steel co. South Chicago, Ill.
Raw and finished material. Free to educational instituti

SUGAR

American sugar refining co. of New York, 117 Wall st. N. Y.
Now preparing an exhibit.

TAPIOCA

Minute tapioca co. Orange, Mass.
Samples of different tapioca products on the market;
exhibit in preparation which will be ready by the first
the year (1915). Free to teachers.

TEA

C. F. Blanke tea and coffee co. 7th and Clark ave. St Louis,
See description of exhibit under coffee. $3.00.

VARNISH

Berry bros. Detroit, Mich.
Limited number of cases, showing specimens of fossil gu
etc. with samples of finished product. Sent on applicat
from principal of school.

VENEER

Acme veneer and lumber co. Cincinnati, O.
Folder of veneer samples. 50c.

WOOD FINISHING

S. C. Johnson and son, Racine, Wis.
Small wood panels finished in different ways. Free.

WOOL

North star woolen mill co. Minn.
Wool in natural state, with steps in manufacturing shown
samples. 25c.

THE NORMAL SCHOOL BULLETIN

EASTERN ILLINOIS STATE NORMAL SCHOOL, CHARLESTON

JULY FIRST, 1916
NUMBER 53

BIRD STUDY IN THE RURAL SCHOOL

by

THOMAS L. HANKINSON, B. S.

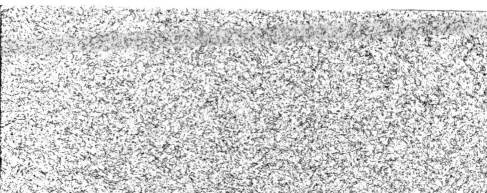

THE NORMAL SCHOOL BULLETIN

Published By The Eastern Illinois State Normal School

Entered March 5, 1902, as second-class matter, at the post office at Charleston, Illinois
Act of Congress, July 16, 1894

CHARLESTON, ILLINOIS. JULY 1, 1916   No. 53

BIRD STUDY IN THE RURAL SCHOOL

by

THOMAS L. HANKINSON

B. S. Michigan State Agricultural College and
Cornell University

Third Edition—Revised and Enlarged

DEPARTMENT OF BIOLOGY, EASTERN ILLINOIS STATE NORMAL SCHOOL

BIRD STUDY IN THE RURAL SCHOOL

The country school, situated in a region rich in natural objects and with pupils, many of whom are at the age when eagerness for knowledge of such objects is best developed, seems to be a place well adapted for nature-study. This subject has made its way slowly, however, into the rural school curriculum. For this there are several reasons, one of which is that many country school teachers are not sufficiently well acquainted with the objects in the natural world about them to enable them to guide their pupils properly in such study. It is the purpose of this article to give the rural school teacher a few directions for independent study of birds, which are particularly well adapted for one who wishes to introduce nature work into a school, and also to give some suggestions that may be helpful in teaching pupils of rural schools about birds.

The study of birds has not only educational value but also considerable interest for most pupils, and it frequently creates a love for wild life generally and forms an attractive avenue to the study of the natural world, where one, if he desires, may select some field for special work. Many men now eminent for their investigations of insects, spiders, shells, mammals, fossils, trees, and other groups of natural objects were led to their present studies by an early interest in birds.

It may seem impossible for a country school teacher, unaided as he is by a museum collection, a large library, or an instructor, to acquire much knowledge of birds, but these handicaps may be considerably overcome by a good field manual or other publication giving descriptions or pictures of birds. A list of the more suitable and readily available works for this purpose are here given.

Bird Guide, Part I, Land birds; Part II, Water birds, by Chester A. Reed. Doubleday, Page & Co., Garden City, N. Y. Part I, 75c; Part II, $1.00.

These are small books that can readily be carried in a pocket. A brief description is given of each species of bird found in Eastern North America, with a simple colored picture of it. These together enable the student to identify the bird when properly seen afield.

Color key to North American Birds, by Frank M. Chapman. Doubleday, Page & Co. $2.50.

This book has an arrangement of colored figures and descriptions of birds similar to that of Reed's Bird Guide, but it is larger and more comprehensive, treating of the birds of all of North America. Teachers who travel much in vacations will find this especially useful.

Birds of New York, by E. H. Eaton. New York State Museum, Albany. Part I, $4.00. Part II, $3.00. Colored plates alone on thin paper. 80c.

These two large quarto volumes with the very complete descriptions and over a hundred colored plates fulfill about all of the requirements for naming our birds, for New York State has a large bird fauna typical of that of Eastern United States generally. The plates are full page size, and each ordinarily shows several species and the different plumages of each species. They are reproductions from drawings made by that skillful bird artist, Mr. Louis Agassiz Fuertes.

Fifty Common Birds of Farm and Orchard, by H. W. Henshaw, Chief of the U. S. Bureau of Biological Survey. Farmer's Bulletin No. 513. Obtained from Sup't. of Documents, Washington, D. C. 15c.

This is a small thirty-one page pamphlet, with brief descriptions and small colored illustrations of fifty of our common birds. Much is given in little space on range, habits, economic status, and other information about each species.

Educational Leaflets. National Association of Audubon Societies, 1974 Broadway, New York. Each 2c.

Each of the eighty-seven leaflets published to date describes and figures, commonly by colored plate, a particular species of bird, making the leaflets very useful for identification purposes.

Bird Charts of the Massachusetts Audubon Society. Prang Educational Co., Boston, Mass. Each $1.50.

These three charts figure life-size in very accurate colors seventy-two of our common birds.

Bird Life, by Frank M. Chapman. D. Appleton & Co. $2.00 for the colored plate edition.

The very good plates and the attractive descriptions are very helpful to one who wishes to know the more common birds.

How to Know the Wild Birds of Illinois, by D. Lange. Educational Publishing Co., Chicago, Illinois. 50c.

This is a small book of pocket size without illustrations but with short descriptions giving distinctive characters in italics. This feature and a simple key makes the look useful as a field manual.

Wild Birds in City Parks, by H. E. and A. H. Walter. A. W. Mumford & Co. Chicago. 40c.

This book has descriptions similar to those in the preceeding book, in that important facts are brought out by a change of type; but it has a unique field key which can be used with considerable success by amateurs.

Handbook of Birds of Eastern North America, by Frank M. Chapman. D. Appleton & Co. $3.50.

This is a standard work on the birds of Eastern North America. Descriptions are given of all the plumages of all the birds of the region. It is an excellent field manual, but some of the smaller books above listed will be found more usable by the beginner. It may be used, however, as an adjunct to these for making field identifications positive.

If possible, bird study should be begun in the winter, for confusion caused by an abundance of species is then avoided. Opera or field glasses are a great aid in observing, but they are not indispensable. All movements in approaching and watching birds should be slow, and the student should avoid wearing brightly colored clothing. One may begin with the study of the birds of the home or school premises if these are large and have plenty of trees, shrubbery, vines, and if they are not too frequently visited by cats, youthful gunners, and other bird enemies. With these proper conditions, judging from observations made about Charleston, most of the following named birds should frequently visit the yard during the winter; all of which are desirable for economic and aesthetic reasons. The ever present English sparrow is, therefore, not listed.

Downy woodpecker	Junco
Red-bellied woodpecker	Tufted titmouse
Flicker	Chickadee
Blue jay	Screech owl
Cardinal	Sparrow hawk
Tree sparrow	

Besides these birds that are almost sure to be present, there are a number that are more irregular in their occurrence, being frequently seen during some winters, ordinarily for short periods only. Such birds are, red-headed woodpecker, yellow-bellied sapsucker, goldfinch, purple finch, white-breasted nuthatch, brown creeper, Carolina wren, cedar waxwing, and mocking bird. Sometimes robins and bronzed grackles arrive very early and are about the yard in the late winter, and once in awhile some of these birds remain over and may be seen about the yard at any time during the cold season. If the barn lot adjoins an open field, horned larks may feed there, especially when the fields are snow-covered. Bob-whites or quails may also come to the yard in severe weather.

One can easily increase the number of birds about one's premises in the winter by placing out food for them. Sweepings from the hay loft and crumbs will attract tree sparrows, juncos, and other seed eaters. Meat rinds, fresh bones broken open or with some meat on them and suet tied to a tree trunk or placed on some support like a veranda roof or feeding shelf made for the purpose will bring downy woodpeckers, nuthatches, chickadees, titmice, blue jays, and perhaps others. A bird's life in winter is often a hard struggle for food, and by supplying this the student is often repaid for his little trouble by the excellent chance he gains of observing bird ways. Attracting birds, however, is an art and one that needs to be studied if much success is to be obtained. The many details cannot be brought out here, but a list of the best publications on the subject known to the writer is here given:

Wild Bird Guests, by Earnest Harold Baynes. E. P. Dutton & Co., New York. $2.15.

This is an up-to-date (1915) treatment of methods and the importance of attracting birds and protecting them.

Methods of Attracting Birds, by Gilbert Trafton, Houghton, Mifflin Co., Boston and New York. $1.25.

The important facts of the subject are brought together by the author of this book after a careful consideration of its rather scattered literature, and the results of the author's many experiences in gaining the friendship of birds are also given.

How to Attract the Birds, by Neltje Blanchan. Doubleday, Page & Co., Garden City, New York. $1.35.

The chapters give ideas as to what can be learned from birds that are encouraged and permitted to dwell about one's home. The first chapter gives good directions on "How to Invite Bird Neighbors."

Our Native Birds, by D. Lange. Macmillan Co., New York. $1.00.

A reading of this little book is very sure to give one an interest in encouraging and protecting birds as well as very good directions for doing this.

How to Attract Birds in Northeastern United States, by W. L. McAtee, Assistant Biologist U. S. Biological Survey, Farmers Bulletin No. 621, U. S. Dep't. of Agriculture. Sup't. of Documents, Gov't. Printing Office, Washington. 5c.

This is a fifteen-page bulletin that gives a large amount of very practical information, including direction for attracting birds.

Plants Useful to Attract Birds and Protect Fruit, by W. L. McAtee. Yearbook of the Department of Agriculture for 1909, pages 185-196. Sup't. of Documents, Gov't. Printing Office, Washington. 5c.

This account appears to give the best information available on ways of attracting birds by properly planting the home or school grounds.

How to Attract and Protect Wild Birds, by Martin Hiesemann. National Association of Audubon Societies, 1974 Broadway, New York. 50c.

This is a small treatise on the very successful ways of attracting birds employed by Baron Von Berlepsch of Germany and the adapation of his methods to American birds.

Attracting Birds About the Home. National Association of

Audubon Societies, 1974 Broadway, New York. 15c. post-paid.

This is a twenty-four page pamphlet made up of a series of short articles by some of the best writers on the subject of bird protection.

Bird Lore, a bi-monthly periodical edited by Frank M. Chapman. D. Appleton & Co., Harrisburg, Pa. $1.00 a year.

This valuable little magazine should be accessible to everyone interested in the birds of this part of the country. Much well-selected new information on ways of protecting and attracting birds as well as other ornithological subjects appears in its columns.

Literature of the Illinois Audubon Society. Obtained from the Secretary, Mrs. F. H. Pattee, 2436 Prairie Ave., Evanston, Illinois. $1.00, which is membership dues.

The Society has just inaugurated "The Audubon Bulletin," which gives promise of being very helpful to bird students in Illinois. Lists of birds, circulars on economic importance and protection of birds, "Educational Leaflets," as well as the "Audubon Bulletin" are distributed free to members.

Although most of our winter birds may be found about the farm yard and about towns and cities, there are some interesting ones that we are not likely to see well unless we take walks in the country. Some of these are the crows that flock in fields and woods and travel to their winter roosts toward evening, the bob-whites that dwell in coveys chiefly about the shrubby growths, mourning doves, sometimes seen in flocks about the corn fields, and prairie chickens, common about corn fields and grassy meadows in some localities. There is always a possibility on these winter field trips of finding individuals of some rare species or some summer resident wintering over, the discovery of either of which gives the bird student a feeling of delight and makes for him a note book record that may be of considerable value.

The early spring is the season when interest in bird study is usually greatest with the beginner, for the birds return from the south about as fast as he can learn them.

To facilitate field work at this time, a list of the common early spring birds of the region about Charleston, Illinois, is here given. They are grouped according to the kinds of places or habitats where the writer usually finds them in the early spring. By early spring is here meant that time from about March 1, when winter seems to have lost its hold and warm days are frequent and the birds begin to return from the south. It lasts till about the middle of April, when spring verdure begins to be prominent.

BIRDS COMMON IN THE EARLY SPRING IN THE REGION ABOUT CHARLESTON, ILLINOIS

Most common in dooryard and orchard:

English sparrow	Bluebird
Robin	Downy woodpecker
Bewick's wren	Mourning dove

Most common in woods, groves and shade trees:

Crow	Cedar waxwing
Blue jay	Tufted titmouse
Sparrow hawk	Chickadee
Flicker	Brown creeper
Red-headed woodpecker	Golden-crowned kinglet
Red-bellied woodpecker	White-breasted nuthatch
Yellow-bellied sapsucker	Myrtle warbler
Hairy woodpecker	Goldfinch
Cowbird	Purple finch
Bronzed grackle	Screech owl

Most common about bushy growths:

Brown thrasher	White-throated sparrow
Cardinal	Junco
Towhee	Phoebe
Field sparrow	Migrant shrike
Fox sparrow	Carolina wren
Song sparrow	Bob-white
Tree sparrow	

Most common in the open field:

Meadow lark	Pectoral sandpiper
Horned lark	Savanna sparrow
Killdeer	Lark sparrow
Upland plover	Vesper sparrow

Most common about bodies of water:

Kingfisher	Red-wing blackbird

In late spring, after about the middle of April, when the

developing foliage becomes conspicious, birds new to the beginner may present themselves in bewildering numbers. Efforts to learn all of these in the first spring of bird study may result in discouragement, so attention would better be directed chiefly to the more common ones during this first season. A list of these that arrive in late spring is here given:

COMMON BIRDS THAT ARRIVE IN LATE APRIL AND IN MAY IN THE CHARLESTON REGION

Most common in dooryard and orchard:

Kingbird	Barn swallow
Orchard oriole	Chimney swift
House wren	Ruby-throated hum-
Chipping sparrow	ming-bird
Purple martin	

Most common in woods, groves and shade trees:

Baltimore oriole	Wood pewee
Rose-breasted grosbeak	Oven bird
Scarlet tanager	Blue-grey gnatcatcher
Summer tanager	Yellow-billed cuckoo
Wood thrush	Red-eyed vireo
Myrtle warbler	Whip-poor-will
Crested flycatcher	

Most common about shrubby growths:

Indigo bunting	Yellow-breasted chat
Maryland yellow-throat	

Most common in open fields:

Dickcissel	Grasshopper sparrow

Most common about bodies of water:

Green heron	Solitary sandpiper
Spotted sandpiper	Water thrush

As summer approaches and the foliage gets thick and the transient and winter-resident birds have gone on north, leaving just the summer residents, identification work becomes more difficult and less interesting. It is now the time to note especially the habits of the birds whose acquaintances were made earlier in the season. Now attention can be concentrated on songs and nesting operations. The woods and fields should be searched for nests, and when one is found it should not be disturbed, for many birds will desert their nests on finding they have been discovered.

For this reason the observer should approach the nest as little as possible, but he should secrete himself as far away as he can and still be able to see the behavior of the birds about it. Field glasses are very useful here, of course.´ The best results can be obtained with a small tent made of brown or green cloth, just large enough to conceal the observer. This can be erected close to the nest, and in a short time birds get accustomed to it and treat it as a stump or other inanimate object. Nest watching under favorable circumstances will show the student much about the domestic habits of birds, the way the nest, eggs, and young are cared for, and the amount and kind of food provided for the latter, the time required for incubation, the period of occupancy of the nest by the young, the development of plumage on them, and the relative amount and kind of attention given to nesting affairs by each parent. Excellent opportunities for making interesting and scientifically valuable photographs are furnished by these nest studies, especially if a blind is used. After the young have left the nest, its structure and position may be studied at close range. In fact, it may be removed for the schoolroom collection, for the birds are through with it. A list of important, available publications on nesting is here given:

Bird Homes, by A. R. Dugmore. Doubleday, Page & Co., Garden City, N. Y. $2.00.

> This is probably the most useful single work on the subject, for it gives many good descriptions and pictures of nests and discusses the general subject of bird nesting in a very thorough way.

Nests and Eggs of North American Birds, by Oliver Davie. David McKay, Philadelphia. $2.25.

> This is an important reference book on the subject, for it gives descriptions of the nests and eggs of all North American Birds.

Home Life of Wild Birds, by F. H. Herrick. Putnam's Sons, New York. $2.00.

> Detailed account of the nesting habits of some of our common birds are given, with very good suggestion for the student who wishes to make such studies himself.

Birds' Nests and Eggs, by Frank M. Chapman. American

Museum of Natural History, New York. Guide Leaflet
No. 14. 10c.

A short, terse general account of birds' nests and eggs
is given and then short descriptions of the nesting site and
the eggs of the birds known to breed near New York City.

Handbook of Birds of Eastern North America, by Frank M.
Chapman. D. Appleton & Co., New York. $3.50.

Pages 66-84 gives a discussion of the nesting season.

This is an excellent treatment of the general subject of
nesting, giving the most important facts known.

Food of Nestling Birds, by Sylvester D. Judd. Yearbook of
the Department of Agriculture for 1900, pages 411-435.
Obtained from Sup't. of Documents, Government Printing
Office, Washington, D. C. 5c.

This treats chiefly of the food of the young of a number
of our common birds, which is information that will be
found useful in connection with field studies.

In all our field work we should not be content with simply
learning the names of birds, though this is necessary as a first
step, and much knowledge of the ways of birds may be obtained
incidentally when names are the chief object. We should find
out all we can about the lives of birds, their favorite habitats,
their food, behavior, nests, economic relations, and so on. A good
way to do this is to take one species at a time and learn as much
as possible about it through both field work and studies of literature. In this way there is a good chance for any student to make
important contributions to the science of ornithology, for little
work of the kind has been done, and each species presents a
field for investigation, the bounds of which no scientist has yet
discovered. For an idea of the possibilities of the intensive
studies see the following:

Monograph of the Flicker, by Frank L. Burns. Published by
the Wilson Bulletin, Oberlin, Ohio. 50c.

As far as possible, knowledge of birds should be obtained at
first hand—that is, by direct observation from nature—but there
is much about them that cannot be learned in this way. Consequently, reading should be done on the general subject of ornithology. The best books for this purpose known to the writer
are here listed. Most of these not only give information but also
a spirit for bird study.

Birds of the World, by F. H. Knowlton and others. Henry
Holt & Co. $7.00.

A very good account of the habits and distribution of birds in general.

The Bird, Its Form and Function, by C. W. Beebe. Henry Holt & Co. $3.50.

Describes in a very readable way the important facts concerning the structure of birds and the uses of their parts.

The Story of the Birds, by James Newton Baskett. D. Appleton & Co., New York. 65c.

A small book with a large amount of information on the structure, functions, and activities of birds.

Birds Through an Opera Glass, by Florence A. Merriam. Houghton, Mifflin Co., Boston, Mass. 75c.

An excellent and interesting account of the habits of our common birds is here given.

Birds Studies With a Camera, by Frank M. Chapman. D. Appleton & Co. $1.75.

Directions for bird photography are given, and also accounts of the habits of some of our most interesting birds.

The Woodpeckers, by Fannie H. Eckstrom. Houghton, Mifflin Co. $1.00.

A very readable account of the most interesting facts concerning this group of birds.

Bird Stories, by John Burroughs. Houghton, Mifflin Co. 60c.

This book is made up of sketches of bird life from the works of John Burroughs. This author uses a vivid style that is bound to stimulate interest in bird life, and his works show the possibilities of careful field observations in getting first-hand information on natural objects.

After the teacher has made some progress in the study of birds he should introduce the subject to his pupils. Little effort will be needed to arouse an interest, for it is present already in most children. Care must be taken, however, especially with boys, to keep the interest properly directed. It should be toward live and free birds and not toward those killed with his gun, and toward eggs in the nest instead of their empty shells in his curiosity collection. A love for the *living* bird should constantly be stimulated by the teacher, which can be done by properly managing the work. Facts concerning the value of birds from an economic and aesthetic standpoint should be presented often.

Bird day may be celebrated, nest boxes may be constructed; food charts and lists of new acquaintances and new arrivals in spring may be put on the blackboard. All of these are good ways of both interesting and instructing pupils in the subject of birds.

Time is usually available for bird work in schools, for it need not have a regular place in the curriculum, but may be indulged in when the pupils need a change from book work, and much fresh air and good muscular exercise may be involved in its pursuit. There are many publications that will give teachers further ideas as to teaching pupils about birds. Some of these that seem especially useful are here given:

Nature Study and Life, by C. F. Hodge. Ginn & Co., Boston. $1.80.

> The chapters on bird studies, comprising about sixty pages, give some of the best directions available for bird work in the schools.

How to Study Birds, by Herbert K. Job. Outing Publishing Co., New York. $1.50.

> Useful suggestions are all through the book, but the final chapter on bird study in the schools is especially important.

Bird Day and How to Prepare for It, by C. A. Babcock. Silver Burdett & Co., Chicago, Illinois. 50c.

> Explicit directions for Bird Day exercises, including suggested programmes, are here given, with much other information useful in teaching work.

Bird Lore, edited by F. M. Chapman. D. Appleton & Co., Harrisburg, Pa. $1.00 a year.

> The School Department of this magazine is designed to help teachers who wish to use birds as materials for nature work. Much help may be obtained from other parts of the periodical.

Nature Study Review, edited by Elliot R. Downing, School of Education, University of Chicago. Comstock Publishing Co., Ithaca, N. Y. $1.00 a year. Published monthly, except in July and August.

> While this periodical deals with nature study in general, there is much on the use of birds in nature work. Some special numbers on the subject have been issued.

What will result from the proper study of birds in the

rural school? The pupil's powers of observation and his aesthetic sense will certainly be cultivated, and a love for birds will be aroused that should cause him always to use his influence for their protection. It is protection that the birds need, for it is very evident from much testimony that birds are becoming less numerous over the greater part of the United States. What effects come from bird destruction? Some important natural enemies of insects are being removed, and the crops are likely to be injured to an increasing extent by these pests. Entomologists estimate that insects cause a loss of over a billion dollars a year to the agricultural and forest interests of the United States. Professor S. A. Forbes, who has made careful studies of both the birds and insects of Illinois, says, "It is true, * * * in my judgement, that the insects of the state of Illinois derive as large a profit from the agriculture of this great state as do the farmers themselves. It is probably true that they cost the state at least half as much as the whole system of public schools." Birds also are of economic value in other ways. Hawks and owls catch the destructive field mice, and on this account, in some localities at least, they are among the most useful of the wild birds. It is true that they catch chickens now and then, and song birds are to some extent destroyed by these birds of prey, but the many food studies that scientists have made make it very evident that enough good is done to make up for these bad habits in all our birds of prey except a very few, only two of which are common and generally distributed in Illinois. These are the Cooper's hawk and the sharp-shinned hawk. Some birds are useful as scavengers and some as destroyers of weed seeds, and some in still other ways. Probably few of us realize how much we owe to them for beautifying the world and adding cheer to our lives through their songs and pleasing activities.

The causes of the very general decrease of our native wild birds have been carefully sought out by scientists. Names and discussions of these can be found in some of the publications listed below. They are given particular attention in those by W. T. Hornaday, who is, in all probability, our best authority on the subject. Some of these are legitimate ones and are due chiefly to the necessary agricultureal processes that make for the progress of civilization, but there are a number of the causes for which good excuses do not exist and are due chiefly to our ignorance of bird life. Few girls would wear wild-bird plumage if they knew the value of the original and rightful owners of this plumage and something of the great amount of destruction of beautiful and interesting birds brought about by this kind of personal adornment. A boy would not be so likely to shoot a song bird if he knew its real value in dollars and cents. Knowledge, then, is what is most needed to give our birds proper protection, and it is especially needed by the farmer, who is probably more directly benefited by birds than anyone else. The rural school teacher is in an excellent position to impart this information to farmers, at least to those who are soon to become farmers. The most useful of the available pieces of literature on this important subject are here listed:

Birds in Their Relation to Man, by C. M. Weed and Ned Dearborn. J. B. Lippincott & Co. $2.50.

This brings the whole subject of the economic importance of our birds up to the time of publication, 1903. Valuable material on bird protection is also given.

Useful Birds and Their Protection, by E. H. Forbush. Massachusetts State Board of Agriculture, State House, Boston. $1.40 postpaid.

This is a well-bound quarto volume of 437 pages, with an extensive and very complete treatment of the subject in general, as well as the special importance of most of the common birds of Eastern North America, since most of these are found in Massachusetts. This state has done much to advance economic ornithology by making an appropriation by which this book can be kept in print and distributed at cost.

Our Vanishing Wild Life, by Wm. T. Hornaday. Charles Scribner's Son. $1.50.

The book is an urgent plea for wild-animal protection, based upon sound data, much of which deals with the economic value of birds.

Wild Game Conservation in Theory and Practice, by Wm. T. Hornaday. Yale University Press. $1.50.

This book also treats of our valuable wild animals,

showing the importance of protecting them and giving much data on their value to man.

The Economic Value of Some Common Illinois Birds, by A. O. Gross and S. A. Forbes. Illinois Arbor and Bird Day Annual for 1909. Office of State Superintendent of Public Instruction, Springfield, Illinois. Free.

This is a short, twenty-page paper containing much information on the more important birds found in Illinois.

Birds in Their Relation to Agriculture in New York State, by A. A. Allen. Cornell Reading Courses, Vol. IV., No. 76. New York State College of Agriculture, Ithaca, N. Y. Free.

This forty-eight page leaflet is an excellent up-to-date (1914) treatment of the economic relations of our common birds. The author's conciseness has enabled him to get many facts into the paper, and these are presented with considerable clearness.

Educational Leaflets. National Association of Audubon Societies, 1974 Broadway, New York. 2c. each.

Each of these leaflets gives the important facts on the economic relations of the bird under consideration.

Publications of the Department of Agriculture, Washington, D. C. Sup't. of Documents, Gov't. Printing Office, Washington, D. C.

There are many bulletins, circulars, reprints, and other Government publications dealing with the economic importance and protection of birds, that can be had at a small cost. Teachers should write to the Superintendent of Documents for a list of these. Some of the recent ones may be obtained free if requests are made to the Editor in Chief, Division of Publications, Washington.

If bird-study is once begun, the pleasure that accompanies it will in most cases insure its continuance. Rarely will it be given up as long as conditions are favorable for its pursuance and if it was begun with any degree of earnestness. There can be no doubt but that the country school teacher and pupils will be well repaid in the way of mental benefit and added pleasure to living if a few hours are taken each week for bird study, and the birds themselves will be benefitted through receiving more of the much-needed protection which a knowledge of them should bring.

EASTERN ILLINOIS STATE NORMAL SCHOOL

THE SCHOOL CALENDAR

1916-1917

FIRST TERM

Nineteen Weeks

September 12, 1916, Tuesday *8:00—12:00 A. M.* *1:30—5:00 P. M.*	*Registration*
December 22, 12:10 Noon *January 2, 7:30 A. M.*	*Holiday Recess*
January 26, 1917, Friday *12:10 Noon*	*First Term ends*

SECOND TERM

Nineteen Weeks

January 30, 1917, Tuesday *8:00—12:00 A. M.* *1:30—5:00 P. M.*	*Registration*
March 30, 12:10 Noon *April 10, 7:30 A. M.*	*Spring Recess*
June 15, 1917 Friday	*Second Term ends*

SUMMER TERM

1917

Six Weeks

June 18, Monday *8:00—12:00 A. M.* *1:30—5:00 P. M.*	*Registration*
July 27, Friday, 12:10 Noon	*Summer Term ends*

THE EASTERN ILLINOIS STATE NORMAL SCHOOL
CHARLESTON

SUMMER SESSION

1917

June 18—July 27

The courses offered will include:

Rural School Methods	Physics
Graded School Methods	Chemistry
Observation	General Science
Psychology	Agriculture
History	Zoology
Government	Physiology
English	Hygiene
German	Botany
Reading	Manual Arts
Music	Mechanical Drawing
Drawing	Domestic Science
Penmanship	Domestic Art
Algebra	Physical Education
Geometry	Athletic Coaching
Geography	Playground Management

Announcements for the summer session will be issued about April first. For information not found in the circular, address President L. C. Lord, Charleston, Illinois.

CPSIA information can be obtained
at www.ICGtesting.com
Printed in the USA
BVHW041343280119
538843BV00005B/103/P